D0934257

Luther College Library
University of Regina

HUSSERL AND PHENOMENOLOGY

Philosophy
—————

Editor
PROFESSOR S. KÖRNER
jur.Dr., Ph.D., F.B.A.
Professor of Philosophy
in the University of Bristol

HUSSERL AND PHENOMENOLOGY

Edo Pivčević
Lecturer in Philosophy
in the University of Bristol

HUTCHINSON UNIVERSITY LIBRARY
LONDON

HUTCHINSON & CO (*Publishers*) LTD
178–202 Great Portland Street, London W1

London Melbourne Sydney
Auckland Johannesburg Cape Town
and agencies throughout the world

First published 1970

The paperback edition of this book is sold subject
to the condition that it shall not, by way of trade
or otherwise, be lent, re-sold, hired out or otherwise circulated without the publisher's prior
consent in any form of binding or cover other than
that in which it is published and without a similar
condition including this condition being imposed
on the subsequent purchaser.

© Edo Pivčević 1970

*This book has been set in Times type, printed in Great Britain
on smooth wove paper by Anchor Press, and
bound by Wm. Brendon, both of Tiptree, Essex*

ISBN 0 09 102980 5 (cased)
0 09 102981 3 (paper)

LUTHER COLLEGE LIBRARY
University of Regina

TO
A.J.AYER

CONTENTS

PREFACE

Edmund Husserl was responsible for setting in motion one of the two main philosophical currents which swept Europe in the first half of this century. One of the chief spiritual initiators of the other was Gottlob Frege. They both were mathematicians but with very different views as to the nature of philosophical method. The problems and difficulties which exercised them still persist and while their teachings no longer attract devoted followers their influence still casts long shadows.

In this book I have tried to explain how Husserl developed his phenomenology from his early 'psychologistic' analysis of number (which brought him into conflict with Frege) to the transcendental phenomenological analysis of his 'mature period'. I have also discussed briefly the views of some other prominent phenomenologists. The phenomenological method has been applied in different contexts and with different results and I have tried to give an illustration of this and also to point out some basic limitations of the phenomenological approach.

I cannot pretend to have given an exhaustive survey of the phenomenological scene. Nor has this been my intention. The sole aim of the book is to provide a brief critical introduction to Husserl and to the ideas of some of the philosophers he influenced, coupled with an invitation to further reading.

My thanks are due to Professor S. Körner, philosophy editor of the Hutchinson University Library, who encouraged me to write this book and helped me with his advice. I am also greatly indebted to Dr C. J. F. Williams who read the manuscript and suggested many improvements, all of which I have incorporated in the final text.

I

AN ANALYSIS 'FREE FROM PRESUPPOSITIONS'

The word 'phenomenology' derives from *phainomenon* (*phainomai*, to appear) and *logos* (reason) and among phenomenologists much significance is attached to this etymology. Whatever 'appears' appears in concrete experiences; there is no 'unexperienced' appearing. Accordingly, the aim of phenomenology is described as the study of experiences with a view to bringing out their 'essences', their underlying 'reason'. This is a very wide definition which tells us nothing about how this study is, or ought to be, pursued, but it gives a sufficient indication as to where the sphere of phenomenological investigations lies. It lies in the domain of *experiences*.

Philosophically the word 'phenomenology' was brought into prominence by Hegel's *Phenomenology of the Spirit* which was published in 1807 and was conceived by Hegel as an introduction to his philosophical system. Hegel was studying the evolutionary pattern of knowledge from the lowest and simplest to the highest and most sophisticated forms of consciousness. In the *Phenomenology of the Spirit* he gave a systematic exposition of these different forms of consciousness presenting them in a world-historical perspective. He interpreted them as stages in the evolution of the 'World Spirit' through World History. He described in his *Phenomenology* the 'journey' of consciousness towards what he called the 'absolute knowledge'; the knowledge, that is, that the Spirit finally gains of its own development, of its own past.

The main idea on which Hegel's system is based is that the 'Absolute' *evolves* by first 'externalising' itself in the world of Nature and then by 'regaining' itself, as it were, at a higher level, through human history and human consciousness. In his system Hegel was recording, so to speak, the 'autobiography' of the Absolute Spirit—the progress of this Spirit towards its full 'self-knowledge'. He was tracing the footprints of God in the world. However, the concept of phenomenology that Husserl introduced in the first decade of this century had a very different meaning from its Hegelian counterpart.

Husserl developed his phenomenology as a method of philosophical analysis free from any *a priori* metaphysical commitment—although, as we shall see later, this method in his own hands became subsequently something much more than just a method. The general purpose of this method, as Husserl originally conceived it, was to exhibit and to elucidate the internal structure of what he called 'experiences of meaning'. Husserl was especially interested in logic and wanted to clarify the basic logical concepts and categories. This, he felt, could not be done satisfactorily without a thoroughgoing inquiry into the nature of meaning. This meant, in the first instance, subjecting the experiences in which we *mean* something or experience something as *meaningful* to close scrutiny so as to bring out the essential features of those experiences. In the pursuit of this task Husserl inevitably came to concern himself more and more closely with the problem of knowledge in general and, as a result, found that he had to widen the scope of his analysis. He began to inquire into the roots of both the logical and epistemological categories and it was to indicate the special nature of his own investigations and their basic differences from what is usually understood by a psychological analysis that he chose for them the name of 'phenomenology'.[1]

We shall have the opportunity, in later chapters, of discussing in some detail the development and the application of the phenomenological method by Husserl and by some of the philosophers he influenced. What is sometimes referred to as the 'phenomenological school' comprises a wide spectrum of differing philosophical views. These differences lead to different emphasis being laid upon, and different values attached to, different classes of experiences. Whereas Husserl, for example, gives pride of place to what he calls 'logical' and 'cognitive' experiences, Scheler and, in a different context, the existential phenomenologists attach primary importance to a phenomenological analysis of emotions. But we shall be in a better position to judge these differences and conflicts if we first examine certain aspects of phenomenology on which there is a considerable measure of agreement.

I have said that experiences are the main objects of phenomeno-

---

[1] At first he tried to familiarise his readers with the new concept by referring to phenomenology as 'descriptive psychology' (as distinct from genetic empirical psychology) but he soon discarded this description as mistaken.

logical interest. Phenomenology is concerned primarily with experiences and their structure; in this, it is conspicuously different from modern Analytic Philosophy which is concerned primarily with the analysis of *propositions*. This, however, does not mean that phenomenology is not interested in language. Quite the contrary, the preoccupation with language is an important feature of phenomenological investigations. But the emphasis remains on experiences. The structure of linguistic expression, it is maintained, cannot be adequately understood without an analysis of the structure of the experiences that makes these expressions meaningful. A sign or a configuration of signs are brought to life in an act of understanding. Without such an act no sign can mean anything.

But one of the chief advantages of basing our analysis on experiences, it is maintained, is that we do not have to begin with any *a priori* and non-evident presuppositions that themselves need explaining. We do not have to make any *a priori* assumptions that require validation outside our field of inquiry. This means that our inquiry will be of a genuinely fundamental kind, and this is precisely what we should aim for if we want to be able to clarify the conditions on which all our knowledge ultimately depends. In natural science we make all kinds of presuppositions. An astronomer describing the movements of planets presupposes the validity of physics, the physicist presupposes the validity of mathematics, the mathematician presupposes the validity of logic, but a phenomenological analysis, it is argued, makes no presuppositions that have to be justified elsewhere. It is more fundamental than any of these disciplines because it is wholly based on what is self-validating and evident; hence its great philosophical value.

There is a clear echo here of Descartes' views on method and the Cartesian inspiration of phenomenology is quite unmistakable. It was Descartes who insisted that philosophy should approach its subject without any prejudices, without any *a priori* assumptions, relying only on what is clearly and distinctly perceived as true. The phenomenologists maintain that the phenomenological method makes just such presuppositionless philosophising possible. It enables us to get to the roots of all problems, to explain their origin and their meaning. A philosophical explanation, it is maintained, unlike an explanation given in natural science for example, has this characteristic: that it does not make any presuppositions that are themselves in need of an explanation. If it does make such presuppositions then, at best, it is not fundamental enough; at the worst, it is dogmatic and uncritical.

Criticism of dogmatism

The view that the phenomenologists are advocating, briefly, is that a philosophical analysis if it wants to be fundamental must be *phenomenological*, i.e. it has to be based on a phenomenological analysis of actual experiences. This explains the aversion that phenomenologists generally feel for traditional metaphysics. In this, there is a certain community of feeling between them and the logical positivists, for all the differences that otherwise divide their respective positions. Both they and the positivists insist that all metaphysical *a priori* assumptions should be eradicated from philosophy and that philosophy should approach its problems in a radically critical spirit. In this respect they have both learned a great deal from Kant. The difference is only that the positivists want to abolish metaphysics altogether, while a considerable number of phenomenologists, just like Kant, aim at providing safe foundations on which a new metaphysics could be built. There is, however, no unanimity in this and in some cases (as we shall see later) the aversion for all kinds of metaphysics persists unabated. But there is certainly a complete agreement in rejecting metaphysical *dogmatism*. Dogmatism is defined as the acceptance, tacit or explicit, of certain metaphysical propositions which have not been properly explained and justified. One such proposition that has come in for a great deal of criticism is that there exists a reality external to, and independent of, the mind —which is the 'natural' realist attitude shared, among others, by the working scientist and the unsophisticated layman. The phenomenologist does not wish to *dispute* the existence of an external world. He only insists that our assertions about the external world should be justified on a phenomenological basis, that is, through a phenomenological analysis of actual experiences. The above proposition, in the form in which it is stated, is, from his point of view, just as dogmatic and phenomenologically indefensible as the assertion of the idealist metaphysician that external things, really, are the product of the mind.

Criticism of dogmatism is not an unfamiliar philosophical pursuit and the phenomenologists are not alone in the field, but they claim to be much more radical than other critics as well as being more consistent. Many philosophers who have criticised dogmatic metaphysical attitudes have themselves resorted to *ad hoc* metaphysical assumptions, thus laying themselves open to the same charges which they were directing against others. It is doubtful whether the phenomenologists themselves are quite free from 'dogmatism' in their approach, but the point they are trying to make about the inconsistencies in earlier philosophical criticism of metaphysics and metaphysical attitudes may be illustrated by two familiar examples, both concerned with the problem of the external world. One comes from Berkeley, the other from Kant.

Berkeley was trying to show that nothing can meaningfully be said about the existence of a world independent of the perceiving mind and that, therefore, the thesis about the 'material substance' must be rejected as dogmatic and uncritical. To assume that sensible objects can exist absolutely 'in themselves', without a mind able to perceive them, is, he maintained, a contradiction, a 'manifest repugnancy'. There can be no meaningful distinction between 'appearances' and a 'thing in itself' as a kind of 'material substratum', the unperceived cause 'behind' appearances. (*'Material substratum* call you it. Pray, by which of your senses came you acquainted with that being?'[1])

Berkeley of course did not wish to deny that sensible things exist when unperceived by ourselves. He only insisted that an explanation be given of the assertion that they do. His argument was that things must be perceived by someone if it is to be meaningful to assert their existence, and since it is (he thought) both natural and reasonable to assume that they do exist when not actually perceived by us, they must be perceived by someone *other* than ourselves, i.e. God. God as the absolute perceiver sustains them in existence.

But the argument, as is obvious, is begging the question; for the inference is based on the assumption that it makes sense to speak of the existence of things when the latter are not actually perceived by us, which itself is justified in terms of the conclusion. The other premiss, namely that things must be perceived by someone if it is to be meaningful to assert their existence, serves only to underline the circularity of the argument.

However, the point Berkeley was trying to make is clear enough. If we accept that it is meaningful to assert the existence of an external world we must be prepared to explain and justify this assertion. We must explain what 'external' means and whether, and in what sense, that which is 'external' can also be described as 'extra-mental'.

Berkeley's way of tackling this problem was to ask the question 'Can we have *knowledge* of something that cannot be perceived?' If, as he believed, all knowledge is either knowledge by direct acquaintance through perception or else it must be definable in terms of such knowledge, then it is clear that all reality, in so far as it can be known and hence meaningfully asserted, must be perceivable. (There is a problem here as to what a perception really consists in, but it would lead us too far to go into this problem now.) The point is that, on this view, we cannot meaningfully assert the existence of

[1] *Three Dialogues between Hylas and Philonous* (First Dialogue).

anything without relating it to the existence of a perceiving mind.

The difficulty, however, is how to explain the possibility of this mind being *different* from one's own. For if there are other minds I cannot know them (in the sense of knowing just explained) however much I may suspect their existence on other grounds. Also I would have to explain spatio-temporal continuity in terms of possible perceptions—my own perceptions. I would have to maintain that all assertions about the world, if they are to be meaningful, must be re-expressible in terms of hypothetical statements about my possible preceptions. It was to avoid these absurdities that Berkeley introduced God. But this hypothesis was of course immediately disqualified by the conditions that he himself imposed on meaningful statements about external reality.

Something similar applies to Kant's doctrine about the 'Thing in itself'. Kant distinguishes between objects of experience (phenomenal objects, things as they appear in experience) and things as they are in themselves, the reality 'underlying' the world of appearances, and because transcending experience, unknowable. But the assumption of a reality of things *per se* is just as much an *ad hoc* metaphysical hypothesis as Berkeley's God. A brief look at the results of Kant's own analysis of the conditions of knowledge will suffice to confirm this.

According to Kant, the area of knowledge extends no further than the area of possible experience. We can *know* things only as phenomenal objects, that is, as objects for us. These objects are in space and time which, according to Kant, are forms of our sense-intuition (and hence not properties of things in themselves) and they (the objects) are subject to certain *a priori* categories and laws which are forms of our understanding. In other words, they are knowable only in so far as they can become objects for a subject of knowledge in accordance with the *a priori* determinable conditions. Nothing that cannot 'appear' as an object in this sense can be known. This inevitably sets limits to the meaningful use of the words 'existence' and 'exists' in relation to things. We shall be justified in saying that something exists as part of the actual world only with regard to the conditions under which it can be *known*. We shall *not* be justified in maintaining the existence of something that cannot become an object of knowledge.

Nevertheless Kant goes on to postulate the 'Thing in itself'. The reasons for this, philosophically inadequate though they are, are not difficult to understand. All phenomenal objects, according to Kant, are constituted in accordance with the laws governing the cognitive faculties of the subject of knowledge. They cannot exist except as thus constituted. Consequently, if we dropped the 'Thing in itself' we would, it seems, be deprived of a truly external world. We would not be able to distinguish between a thing *qua* thing and a thing *qua* object of someone's cognitive consciousness and this would make it difficult to speak of things existing when they are not objects of anyone's cognitive consciousness. The concept of the 'Thing in itself', in fact, was introduced by Kant to emphasise that there is a reality genuinely independent of the cognitive mind. However, the difficulty was that this hypothesis was vitiated by the conditions that he himself imposed on the meaningful assertion of existence.

Phenomenological constitution and logical construction

The phenomenologists are severely critical of all such *ad hoc* metaphysical hypotheses and indeed of all assumptions that cannot be explained in phenomenological terms. From the phenomenological standpoint the doctrine of the 'Thing in itself' is unacceptable and Husserl certainly loses no time in repudiating it. It is unacceptable because it implies that what actually 'appears' in experience is not the real thing, that the phenomenal object is merely a stand-in for something else that remains transcendent to every experience. But to assume that there is a reality which is never disclosed in experience is phenomenologically inadmissable. Phenomenology, in a sense, is closer to empiricism than Kant ever was. However, having said this I must add that 'closer' here still involves a considerable distance and that Husserl especially showed, as his phenomenological investigations progressed, an ever increasing Kantian influence. Whilst remaining critical of the 'Thing in itself' he found Kant's transcendental argument appealing and eventually developed his own version of the 'transcendental method'.

But leaving a detailed analysis of Husserl's philosophical development for later, I want to make a few general remarks about the concept of *phenomenological constitution* which is one of the basic concepts of phenomenology. Phenomenology is said to make no *a priori* presuppositions. It is said to start its analysis with concrete experiences distilling out what is essential and basic in those experiences. It conducts its analysis without making any dogmatic assumptions, without any metaphysical bias, its aims being to establish the basic and incontrovertible phenomenological facts. But what are these facts and what do we do with them? Can we, starting from these facts, 'reconstruct' the world in phenomenological terms? How do we advance from subjective experiences where our analysis must begin to an objective world which we share with other people? How do we explain the possibility of an objective order? Furthermore, we normally accept that there are things which we cannot experience in any direct sense, such as someone else's pain; but how can we account for the possibility of experiences different from our own? How can I explain in phenomenological terms the possibility of 'other egos'? These and related problems are the problems of 'phenomenological constitution'. The task of 'phenomenological constitution' is to show how all these things are possible. It would indeed be of little use to put so much emphasis on concrete experiences if we were not able, by analysing the structure of such experiences, to explain the basic features of the world we live in. Besides, failure to provide such an explanation would throw serious doubts on the claim that phenomenological analysis is 'free from presuppositions'. Consequently, a phenomenologist, if he wants to be consistent, has no alternative but to try to show that a 'phenomenological constitution' of complex higher-order objects on the basis of what is found in concrete experiences is indeed possible. He must try, in short, to 'reconstruct' the world on a phenomenological basis.

At this point yet another comparison with modern positivism seems to obtrude itself. The concept of 'phenomenological constitution' brings to mind the concept of 'logical construction' which modern positivists use so frequently. Their aim is to try and show that the world can be explained as a logical construction out of certain basic elements. These elements are interpreted sometimes as 'sense-data', sometimes as 'sense-contents' and sometimes as 'elementary experiences'. The concept of construction was taken over from mathematics and its origin largely determined its meaning. In mathematics the basic elements are represented by the series of positive integers from which the whole number system can be derived by construction. Starting with 1, 2, 3, . . . we can construct the negative numbers, the rational numbers, the real numbers, and so on. The positivists believed that something similar can be done in epistemology. They tried to show that all objects of pre-scientific and scientific knowledge can be constructed out of certain basic elements, or, more precisely, that they can be *defined* in terms of such elements with the help of certain primitive concepts. The most notable attempt at such a construction was made by Carnap in 1928 in his book *Der logische Aufbau der Welt* (*The Logical Structure of the World*). Carnap used *experiences* as his basic elements and just one primitive concept—'recollection of similarity' (similarity between 'elementary experiences'). He tried to show that from this austere basis everything else can be derived (explained) by logical construction: the various sense qualities, spatial and temporal order, the world of physical objects, other persons, cultural objects, etc. According to Carnap, the basic elements for such a construction are to be found in my own 'stream of experiences' (Erlebnisstrom)—although, as he points out, the expression 'my own', strictly speaking, should not be used until the object to which this expression refers has itself been constructed. The 'self' is not included among what is originally given and has to be constructed as a class of elementary experiences. I shall not discuss the question whether such a programme of construction can actually be carried out or not. The positivists themselves no longer believe that radical constructivism is a tenable position and since the publication of the *Aufbau* Carnap has found compelling reasons for revising his earlier views. The interesting thing here is that both the programme of phenomenological constitution and the positivist programme of logical construction (at least as it is conceived in the *Aufbau*) are designed to rid philosophy of *a priori* metaphysical assumptions and that both use experiences as a basis.

But there is an important difference. The experiences that the phenomenologist (a Husserlian phenomenologist at least) is interested in are what he calls 'intentional experiences' or 'acts'. Every such experience, it is said, has the property of being a 'consciousness of something', of being 'intentionally related to something'. I shall deal with the problem of intentionality in detail in Chapter 4. The important thing to point out here is that the concept of an experience with which the phenomenologist is concerned involves what Husserl calls an 'act of consciousness'. Experiences can be cognitive and 'reflective' or 'non-reflective' like sensations, but they are all *conscious* experiences. The positivist denies the presence of any kind of duality in 'elementary experiences' and looks at them as simple elements which cannot be further analysed. All dualist distinctions, from his point of view, can be explained as a result of logical construction. The phenomenologist, on the other hand, sees experiences, all experiences, as having an internal structure which can be adequately explored only *from the inside*. If we want to explain the presuppositions of knowledge we must study cognitive experiences and cognitive experiences are not just events like other events; they are *object-constituting* events. They have an 'intentional structure' and this structure, the phenomenologist maintains, can be explored in 'reflective consciousness' or 'inner perception'. Consequently, he argues that a 'phenomenological constitution' (a philosophical 'reconstruction') of the world must be based not on a 'logical construction' in the positivist sense but on a *phenomenological analysis* of experiences.

What kind of beginning?

However, the difficulties involved in carrying out a programme of 'phenomenological constitution' are no less formidable than those involved in carrying out a programme of positivist construction and their consequences are just as far-reaching. In fact, both the phenomenologist and the positivist, each within his own theoretical context, are faced with very much the same kind of dilemma: they must either widen the *bases* of their respective programmes and use more liberal methods of 'construction' or they must simply admit that a very large number of problems cannot be solved from their respective positions. But to widen the basis would mean, in practical terms, introducing new concepts, new postulates, new initial assumptions, and, in the case of the phenomenologist, it would mean accepting presuppositions that are *not* self-validating. All this is exactly the opposite of what was originally intended.

The problem, briefly, is one of deciding what our starting assumptions are going to be; how we choose the principles with which to begin our philosophical reconstruction of the world and how we make sure that these principles are really adequate. It is a problem of *where* to begin and *how* to begin and this problem has been acute in European philosophy since Descartes.

Descartes was searching for a philosophical 'Archimedean point' from which the whole world could be 'heaved', as it were, into the light of reason, and he believed that he had found this in *cogito ergo sum*—I think, therefore I am. Here—he thought—there was something which was absolutely fundamental and absolutely indubitable, an axiom on which a rational explanation of the world could, and indeed should, be based. But his 'axiom' could not fulfil this role if only because it assumed more things than it explained. It assumed that the fact of thoughts occurring is a sufficient evidence from which to infer the existence of a thinking thing. To Descartes the 'axiom' was a proof that I exist as a 'thinking substance' essentially different from 'extended matter'. But the 'axiom' was nothing of the kind. From the fact that I think, i.e. the fact that something is an object of my thought, nothing can be inferred either about the existence of a 'substantival ego' or about the reality of the object of my thought; it can only be inferred that there exists an experience of a particular type. Descartes' 'axiom' was not as axiomatic as he believed it to be. So far from being self-validating the assertion 'I think, therefore I am' tacitly presupposes the general premiss 'Everything which thinks, exists' which has yet to be proved.

Descartes' 'axiom' obviously was not a satisfactory beginning. But perhaps this was due only to Descartes mistaking the true meaning of '*cogito*'. Descartes erroneously assumed that '*cogito*' could serve as a basis for drawing metaphysical inferences. He made assertions which went far beyond the evidence supplied by the simple fact that 'I think'. But suppose we manage to avoid his mistakes.

Suppose we are careful to avoid all metaphysical assumptions, confining our attention solely to the 'phenomenological content' of the *cogito*, i.e. to the relation of consciousness to its object. Could we not use the *cogito* in this form as a basis for a 'phenomenological reconstruction' of the world?

This is the sort of question that a sympathetic critic of Descartes might ask, but the difficulty is that having suggested this possibility he is immediately faced with a new problem. The *cogito* embraces all types of conscious experiences. Which experiences should we start with? Which experiences are fundamental? It seems clear that our choice of experiences and the manner in which we interpret these experiences must depend on the kind of initial assumptions we make. These assumptions will not be self-validating but will receive whatever justification they have from the success of the explanation based on them. But if this is so, if we accept that there is a need for such assumptions, what sense can be made of the idea of 'presupposition-less philosophising?'

This is the problem phenomenology is facing and, not unnaturally, finding difficult to solve.

In what follows, I shall first examine Husserl's philosophical development. I shall then explain briefly the main ideas of Scheler's anthropology which will throw some light on the controversial problem of the relations between phenomenology and anthropology. Finally, I shall discuss the views of Heidegger and Sartre.

2

HUSSERL'S CONCEPTION OF NUMBER AND
HIS CLASH WITH FREGE

Husserl began his career as a mathematician and his early philosophical interests were closely connected with mathematics. He studied
mathematics under the famous mathematicians Weierstrass and
Kronecker between 1878 and 1881 and after completing his doctoral
dissertation on the calculus of variations he worked for a time as an
assistant to Weierstrass at Berlin University. Mathematics at that time
was making big advances but the research into its foundations was
only just beginning and already deep disagreements were clouding
the horizon. Some clarity was urgently needed and the young Husserl
was determined to make his own contribution towards this end.

Pure Arithmetic, he heard his teacher Weierstrass emphasise in
his lectures, is a science based simply and solely on the concept of
number and apart from this it needs no other presuppositions, no
other postulates or premisses. But what is number; how do we make
clear the meaning of the concept of number? The new theories by
Georg Cantor concerning transfinite numbers which were the object
of much heated discussion at the time gave this question an added
urgency. How far does the realm of numbers extend? Are we to
accept transfinite as well as finite numbers? Are we to assume that
the existence of a number, in certain cases, can be asserted on the
basis of logical considerations only, without our being able actually
to construct such a number? Cantor thought so, but this view was
not very popular among mathematicians. Kronecker, who was one
of Cantor's leading opponents, maintained that the introduction of
transfinite numbers by such methods was entirely illegitimate. All
mathematical objects, he maintained, are obtained by construction

from positive whole numbers. There are no other basic numbers but these. But if the whole of mathematics could be derived by construction from positive integers or 'natural numbers' the problem still remained of how to explain these 'natural numbers'. What is a 'natural number'? Obviously, this question could not be answered within mathematics proper. An explanation had to be attempted in other than purely constructivist terms. It was necessary to start looking beyond mathematics proper towards the latter's 'non-mathematical presuppositions'.

In 1884, when Husserl was twenty-five, Gottlob Frege, who was eleven years his senior and a professor of mathematics at Jena, published his *Foundations of Arithmetic* (*Die Grundlagen der Arithmetik*) in which he attempted to do just this. Husserl who was working on the same problem presented his views in his *Habilitationsschrift* in 1887 and then in an expanded version in 1891 in his *Philosophy of Arithmetic* (*Philosophie der Arithmetik*). Both he and Frege in their inquiries into numbers had one overriding aim: to clarify the basic *presuppositions* of mathematics. But in the pursuit of this aim they followed very different paths. Their views clashed, and in order to understand Husserl's philosophical development it is necessary to examine the causes and the consequences of his conflict with Frege.

Husserl was profoundly influenced by Franz Brentano's descriptive psychological method of analysis and it was from a descriptive psychological standpoint that he began his analysis of number. Feeling uncertain about continuing his career as a mathematician he came to Vienna to study philosophy under Brentano who made a profound impact on him and influenced his whole intellectual development. Husserl accepted Brentano's method of analysis and tried to apply this method to mathematical concepts. He wanted to clarify what he called the 'origin' of the concept of number and sought help from psychology. Frege, on the other hand, was trying to explain the logical presuppositions of mathematics and was interested primarily in *definitions*.

This was the source of the conflict. Husserl regarded Frege's logicist analysis as unsatisfactory and incapable of getting to the root of the problem, and in his *Philosophy of Arithmetic* he sharply attacked Frege's view of numbers and Frege's general anti-psychologistic position. He did not think that the concept of number could be given a logical *definition*. Logically simple concepts such as the concept of a plurality, the concept of unity, the concept of something, etc.—he maintained—cannot be 'defined' in the ordinary sense and this equally applies to the concept of number which is closely connected with these concepts. All we can do is to try and explain how we acquire these concepts, and this, Husserl insisted, requires a descriptive psychological analysis.

However, partly no doubt under the influence of Frege's criticism (expressed in a long review of his book) and partly as a result of the difficulties he encountered in his own further research into mathematical theory, he became convinced of the inadequacy of the psychologistic approach and eventually changed course. The result was his famous book *Logical Investigations* (*Logische Untersuchungen*) the first volume of which appreared in 1900. In this, he retracted[1] his criticism of Frege's anti-psychologism. But although now an anti-psychologist himself he steered in a direction very different from the one Frege took. Frege's method of logical definitions did not appeal to him and whilst criticising psychologism he continued his descriptive analysis of meaning at a more 'purified' phenomenological level. In 1901 he published the second volume of *Investigations* in which he laid the foundations of his philosophical phenomenology. This was an altogether different book from Frege's main work *Fundamental Laws of Arithmetic* (*Grundgesetze der Arithmetik*) of which the second and last volume appeared only two years later.[2]

These two books are two major landmarks in the development of modern European philosophy. In his *Grundgesetze* Frege applied in a systematic form the ideas he developed earlier in his *Foundations of Arithmetic*; but his views, at first, did not arouse much interest and it was mainly through Russell and the latter's modified version of his—Frege's—logicist programme that his influence began to spread. Husserl's book, on the other hand, made an immediate impact on the philosophical public on the Continent and was widely regarded as having conclusively proved the untenability of the psychologistic position in logic. His book showed at the same time that he had finally lost active interest in the problems connected purely with mathematics.

The epistemological v. the logical approach

But the reasons why Husserl developed in a different direction will become clearer if we examine his theory of numbers and his conflict with Frege a little more closely. His early position, although subsequently criticised by Husserl himself as 'psychologistic', provides important clues to his later views and a comparison between his and Frege's views will help an understanding of the basic differences between the 'phenomenological method' (which he developed later) and the method of logico-linguistic analysis used by Frege and his followers. It will also illustrate a problem which every inquirer into

[1] In a footnote.
[2] The first volume of *Grundgesetze* appeared in 1893.

numbers seems destined to face at some time or other. The problem concerns the discrepancy between the *noetic*[1] and the *logical* categories, or, to put it differently, the discrepancy between the epistemological and the logical aspect of knowledge. He must either try to reconcile these two aspects or decide which of them to explore. But to reconcile these two aspects is far from easy. It is probably not possible at all, unless we are prepared to accept certain metaphysical assumptions which create difficulties of their own. And to limit one's investigation to one aspect only means, in effect, giving up the attempt to grasp the problem in its entirety, and this can only lead to unsatisfactory simplifications.

It is one of the peculiarities of numbers that they give rise to this problem and thereby force the philosophically minded mathematician to extend his inquiry to a much wider philosophical field. Husserl soon found that he had to broaden the basis of his inquiry. Frege, too, in the course of his analysis had to touch on some wider philosophical issues. But while Frege's main preoccupation was to explore the logical presuppositions of mathematical knowledge and to 'reconstruct' mathematics on a logical basis, Husserl was interested in the noetic presuppositions of both mathematics and logic. Frege studied the problems of logical relations and logical structure of mathematical statements. Husserl was interested primarily in problems of origin and meaning.

Both Frege and Husserl studied the problems of a theory of formal deductive systems, but they did this from rather different angles. Frege was more concerned with the internal logical structure of such a theory. Husserl was predominantly interested in its general philosophical foundations. Frege tried to set up a consistent logical system of general arithmetic. Husserl inquired into the philosophical basis of logic. Mathematico-logical problems opened a wide front of fundamental philosophical issues. Unlike Frege, Husserl decided that they should be pursued with much more tenacity outside the strictly logico-mathematical sphere. He was interested in their noetic background. This, however, does not mean that he was against mathematical logic. On the contrary, in his *Logical Investigations* he writes: 'Not the mathematician, but the philosopher is outside his natural rights when he resists the "mathematically-oriented" theories of logic and refuses to hand his temporary foster children to their natural parents. The derogatory tone in which the philosophical logicians like to speak about the mathematical theories of inference does not in the least alter the fact that the mathematical

---

[1] We shall often use this term in explaining Husserl's views. It is a term that he himself uses very frequently. The meaning of 'noetic' is close to that of 'cognitive'.

form of procedure in these, as in all other rigorously developed theories (one must of course take this word in its real sense), is the only scientific one ...'[1]

But while thus fully acknowledging the value of mathematical logic, Husserl points out at the same time that mathematical logic is utterly incapable of dealing with many vital logico-philosophical problems. What he finds impressive about the new logic is its strictly deductive structure, its systematic character, its rigorous methods. All the same, he thinks these admirable qualities of the new logic cannot conceal the fact that this logic, philosophically, suffers from serious limitations. There is too much emphasis on calculus and too little on meaning. Logical calculus may be a useful instrument but only if we are clear about the meaning of the presuppositions on which it is based and this meaning is a matter for philosophical analysis. To Husserl, a mathematician is only an 'ingenious techni-cian' who constructs his logico-mathematical theory like a 'technical work of art', by adhering strictly and exclusively to the formal rules of implication. The philosopher goes much deeper than this: he asks what is the essence of theory as such, what are the basic laws and basic concepts underlying theory-construction; in short, what makes a theory a *theory*. He is not so much interested in the specific methodological problems that might be encountered in particular sciences as in the theoretical conditions that make science what it is. His aim, according to Husserl, is, or at any rate ought to be, to provide a philosophical theory of science, a *Wissenschafts-lehre*.

The differences between Husserl's line of approach and Frege's logical analysis indicate a deeper conflict of theoretical attitudes— a conflict which later became progressively more apparent as they and their followers continued to develop and apply their respective methods of inquiry. Analytic philosophy laid the main emphasis on contextual logical analysis and came to regard ontology merely as an *extension of logic*—and a contextual and pragmatic extension at that. Phenomenology, on the other hand, with its emphasis on origin and meaning prepared the way for a new ontology as a fundamental philosophical discipline with logic proper receding gradually into the background. We shall have to say more about this later on. We must first examine the basic ideas of Husserl's theory of numbers as put forward in his *Philosophy of Arithmetic*; for psychologistic as it certainly is this early work by Husserl, besides being a valuable contribution to the discussion about num-bers, shows already especially in the treatment of relations signs of an attitude which will (in spite of his subsequent rejection of psycho-

[1] *Logische Untersuchungen*, 3rd ed., vol. I, p. 253.

logism) guide his thoughts eventually into channels very different from those of the logico-linguistic analysis inspired by Frege.

Numbers, concepts and mental acts

In his *Philosophy of Arithmetic* (which, incidentally, is subtitled 'Psychological and Logical Investigations') Husserl set himself a twofold task. His aim was, first, to explore the psychological background to the concept of number (cardinal number, *Anzahl*). Secondly, he wanted to examine what he regarded as the logical aspects of number-construction within a given symbolic system of numbers; for 'all ideas that we have of the numbers other than the first few in the number series, are symbolic; this fact determines completely the character, the meaning and the purpose of arithmetic'.[1] Arithmetic operates with concrete, tangible signs. It might be possible to interpret the process of construction of numbers from other numbers as a conceptual operation in which the signs play a subordinate role. But the method by which we construct numbers as signs from other signs according to certain rules is, in Husserl's opinion, vastly superior to the 'conceptual method'. It is less abstract and much handier to use.

This might give the impression that Husserl advocates a kind of constructivist formalism in arithmetic. However this is not so. His 'operational' view of arithmetic does not, for example, prevent him from speaking of the numbers within a particular number-system (*systematischen Zahlen*) as representatives of the numbers 'in themselves' (*Zahlen an sich*). His main concern was, first, to show the indispensability, and indeed the handiness, of the ordinary arithmetical symbolism; and, secondly, to stress the role of arithmetical operations in the formation of arithmetical concepts. It was obvious to him that a close study of arithmetical methods of construction was of fundamental importance, and this, in fact, was to have been the subject of the second volume of the *Philosophy of Arithmetic* which never appeared. The problems Husserl encountered in his effort to develop a system of 'general arithmetic' led him to expand his inquiry beyond the strictly mathematical field and change some of his previously held views. One of the casualties of this change was the 'psychologistic' explanation of numbers which he gave in the first part of the *Philosophy of Arithmetic* and which I shall now discuss briefly.

The concept with which we are here concerned is of course that of *cardinal* number. It is this concept that Husserl at first tried to explain from what he subsequently criticised as the 'psychologistic position', although this position, as we shall see, contained many

[1] *Philosophie der Arithmetik* (Halle Saale, 1891), p. 212.

elements which, phenomenologically 'purified', later reappeared in his 'transcendental phenomenology'. The chief difference between his and Frege's view of number can be briefly expressed by saying that while Frege tried to explain number in terms of extensions of concepts, Husserl tried to give a descriptive psychological analysis of its 'genesis'. The main concepts which Frege used in his analysis were 'extension', 'equinumerosity' (or extensional equality, *Gleichzahligkeit*) and 'one-one correspondence'. It is these concepts that form the basis of Frege's logical definitions. Husserl, as we saw, distrusts definitions and inquires into the 'origin' of the concept of number. His main concepts are 'collective' (an arbitrary aggregate of objects), 'plurality', 'mental acts' and what he calls 'collective association' (*kollektive Verbindung*).

These two sets of concepts reveal already the deep contrast between their respective positions. Yet, curiously enough, despite the fundamental differences in their attitudes there are certain points, not altogether unimportant, on which they are both in agreement. *First*, they both criticise the view that numbers can be explained from the intuition of time. Frege points out (as did J. F. Herbart, who to a considerable extent anticipated his logical theory of numbers) that time has nothing to do with the concept of number, that it is only a psychological necessity for *counting*. Husserl fully agrees with this, although not quite for the same reasons. The mere fact of temporal succession, he says, is not enough to produce a collection of objects. For this, we need a *synthetic mental act*. The unity of a collective whole is based on such an act and not on an experience of time. *Secondly*, both Frege and Husserl criticise the formalists who tend to confuse numbers with signs. A number—they both point out—is not a mere collection of '1's. Counting, says Husserl, would be entirely meaningless if the sign '1' were not associated with the concept *one*, and he criticises the nominalistic view of numbers (held, among others, by Berkeley) according to which signs are to be regarded as the fundamental objects of arithmetic. *Thirdly*, both Husserl and Frege agree that numbers are not obtained through straightforward abstraction from things and both are critical of J. S. Mill's view that the 'fact asserted in a definition of a number is a physical fact'—although Husserl, at this stage, finds Mill in some other respects a congenial thinker.

However, all these remarkable agreements cannot obscure the fact that Husserl and Frege, in essentials, remain wide apart in their views. The deep gulf that divides their positions is largely the result of their different handling of a concept which is both logically and philosophically of fundamental importance—the concept of *relation*. The differences in their treatment of this concept played a decisive role in both their own philosophical development and the development of the schools which their teachings inspired.

In his analysis of relations Husserl depended essentially on Brentano. According to him, there are two classes of basic relations. One of these comprises the so-called 'primary relations'; these relations are connected with what Brentano called 'physical phenomena', but, Husserl points out, they are not necessarily confined to what is usually understood by 'physical objects'. The main characteristic of a 'primary relation', he says, is that it is immediately recognised as a constitutive part of the idea that we have of the related terms. It is given, as it were, together with its terms. Primary relations include the relations of similarity, equality, degree (*Steigerung*), etc. Then, there is a second class of relations: the relations which, unlike the 'primary relations', have the character of 'mental phenomena'. These relations, says Husserl, are based on mental, intentional acts, such as the acts of imagining, judging, willing, emotional acts, etc. The objects are here brought into relation with each other in virtue of such *acts* and the relation can be detected only through reflection upon such acts.[1]

It is to this second class of relations that Husserl attaches special importance. Later in the course of his philosophical development he will—although at a different level—revert once again to the analysis of intentional relations, combining his new phenomenological concept of intentionality with a criticism of psychologism. But we shall have an opportunity of discussing this later on. Now we must find out in what way these so-called 'mental relations' bear upon the problem of numbers.

We said that one of Husserl's basic concepts is that of a *collective*. A collective comes into being as a result of our focusing attention upon certain objects and associating them into a group. It can contain widely differing members which need not be either temporally or spatially connected. The only nexus between them is that of a 'collective association'. This 'collective association', according

---

[1] It might be helpful to quote Husserl's own explanation of the difference between these two classes of relations. 'One can describe the characteristic difference between the two classes of relations . . .'—he writes— 'by saying that whereas the primary relations as objects of presentations belong, in a sense, to the same level as their terms, this is not so with mental relations. In the case of primary relations the relation is given together with its terms as part of the same content of presentation. In the case of mental relations however, the relation can become an object of presentation only as a result of a reflection on the act that sets it up. The immediate object of reflection is the act itself; it is only after we have made this act an object of our reflection that we are in a position to consider the terms of the relation. The terms and the relation belong thus, in a sense, to different levels.' *Philosophie der Arithmetik*, p. 74.

to Husserl, is a *mental relation* and involves a synthetic mental act. It is a type of connexion entirely different from the kind of connexion encountered, for example, in *perception*. Perceptual connexions are regarded by Husserl as 'primary connexions'. A perceptual complex—my perception, say, of the vase of flowers on my desk—exhibits a 'primary connexion' in the sense that whilst being 'analysable' into parts it possesses nevertheless an original unity. The situation is different in the case of 'collective association'. Here, according to Husserl, the unity is effected only as a result of a synthetic mental act. By reflecting on this act and by concentrating on the aspect of the collective association in a given collective, Husserl maintains, we obtain the abstract concept of a plurality (*Vielheit*). Only a short step divides us now from numbers. For while concentrating our attention on the aspect of the collective association we can at the same time stop attending to objects as individuals with their particular properties and regard each of them merely as *something*. This will result in an abstract plurality of something and something and something, etc., or one and one and one, etc., of which determined 'segments' such as one and one, one and one, and one, are numbers.

To sum up, Husserl's view is that the collective association binds objects into groups of countable units. This collective association is a mental relation because it is based on a *mental act*. In his view, it is necessary to introduce mental acts and mental relations because no 'primary relation' can explain how the most diverse objects can be assembled together and counted. The act by which the collective association is established is followed by a process of abstraction and this, according to his explanation, yields us the concepts of particular numbers.

Frege's criticism of this view

Frege rejects this analysis completely. He regards Husserl's reasoning as psychologistic and somewhat naïve. How is Husserl to explain the number one or the meaning of zero on his premises? Clearly, in these cases there can be no 'collective association' for there is no collective. Here we cannot rely on any 'mental acts' and the only solution, according to Frege, is to attempt an explanation in terms of *extensions of concepts*. We shall have to explain *one* in terms of extensional equality of concepts under which only one object falls, and *zero* in terms of extensional equality of concepts under which no object falls. Husserl based his analysis of numbers on the idea of a collective and the idea of a collective association and, naturally, tried to play down the importance of relations such as extensional equality or one-one correspondence. But, according to Frege, it is on these relations that we should base an explanation of number and not on any analysis of 'mental acts'.

Frege's view, briefly, is that numbers attach to *concepts*. It is through concepts that objects are counted. The concept defines the *domain* of counting. An object or group of objects can be viewed from different aspects, that is, in different conceptual contexts, and, as a result we may get different collections of different units. As Frege points out, the *Iliad* can be viewed either as one book or as a collection of twenty-four books, or for that matter as a very large collection of verses. The result of counting will thus always depend on the *nature of the concept*. A concept may be such that just one object falls under it (e.g. the concept 'Moon of the Earth'), or it may be such that nothing whatever falls under it (e.g. 'Man with two heads'); which makes it possible to explain the meaning of one and zero. The concept, maintains Frege, is the 'bearer of number'. A statement of number in reply to 'how many?' involves an assertion about a concept.

But let us pursue Frege's view a little further. Since he believes that a statement of number (in reply to 'how many?') involves an assertion about a concept, he naturally regards the analysis of the meaning of such an assertion as his main task. In order to explain the meaning of number he must explain what it means to assert that a number applies to a certain concept. The problem for him, as he sees it, is one of clarifying the meaning of the expression 'The number which applies to the concept F'. He relies for this clarification on the relations of equinumerosity and one-one correspondence (which Husserl, incidentally, would class among 'primary relations'). The definition he finally arrives at is somewhat complicated.[1] Its meaning, basically, is this: that the number applicable to a given concept can be explained in terms of *coextensiveness* or *extensional equality* with that concept. If, for example, the concept F is such that just one object falls under it—let F be, say, 'planet between Venus and Mars', there being, as it happens, only one such object—then 'equinumerous with F' will, according to Frege, represent a concept whose extension is the *number one*.

Unlike Husserl then who favours a 'genetic' approach to numbers, Frege pursues a purely logical line of inquiry. Their methods are radically different. They have different conceptions of what is presupposed in a statement of number and whereas Husserl insists on the importance of the 'collective association' and synthetic mental

---

[1] Here it is: 'The number which applies to the concept F is the extension of the concept "equinumerous with the concept F".' It should only be added that 'equinumerous' means 'extensionally equal' or 'coextensive' and is eventually itself defined in terms of one-one correspondence.

acts Frege places the main emphasis on the extensional analysis of concepts.

Some limitations of the two theories

Both these theories have serious weaknesses, although Husserl's theory, epistemologically speaking, has certain advantages. It has the attraction of providing a readily intelligible philosophical analysis of the 'evolution' of arithmetical concepts instead of merely replacing the arithmetical concepts by logical concepts which, philosophically, are just as obscure. Frege's logical analysis, for all its subtlety and technical precision, remains philosophically unsatisfying. It certainly begs many questions. Frege rests his explanation of numbers on the concept of extensional equality and presupposes that we already understand what 'extension of a concept' means. However, this is something that requires an explanation. Furthermore, it is not at all clear how the extensional equality of a set of otherwise completely unrelated concepts is to be established. In the case of non-empty concepts we may be able to pair off the objects falling under these concepts in one-to-one fashion. But this procedure will not work in the case of empty concepts. For example, how do we establish the extensional equality between the concept 'green Pegasus' and the concept 'invisible man'? Before we can do this we must come to an agreement as to the meaning of 'non-existence' and this raises difficult problems that have nothing to do with logic.

But suppose the problem of extensional correlation between concepts raises no unsurmountable difficulties. Suppose we have succeeded in making the meaning of extensional equality sufficiently clear by showing that there are relations which do in fact correlate concepts in such a way that their extensional equality becomes immediately apparent. This will still not be enough to explain the meaning of number unless we have shown how the extensions of any two concepts thus correlated can be interpreted as instances of the same class of extensions. For we do not want merely to be able to say that two concepts are extensionally equal but that the same number applies to both of them. More clearly, we do not want to say merely that there are just as many apples on the table as there are eggs in the basket, but that the *number* of apples is the *same* as the number of eggs.

It is these and similar considerations that led Frege to regard numbers as objects in their own right, forming part of the basic 'furniture of the world'. But this view, as subsequent logicians have shown, can be imported into logic only on pain of contradictions. There is no doubt that the exclusion of zero and one represents a serious defect in Husserl's theory. But it is also not very helpful to regard them, along with other numbers, as objects, as Frege does. In fact, both Frege's and Husserl's theory have many weak points and neither can be said to give a satisfactory explanation of numbers.

What is for us of special interest here is of course the general premisses from which they approach the subject of their inquiry, for these premisses have a wider philosophical significance. Frege's guiding principle is the relation of equality and one of the main objects of his analysis is to find out how this relation works in the logico-mathematical context. He studies the meaning of mathematical equation. He tries to clarify the meaning of logical equivalence. He speaks of numbers as objects, but he is primarily interested in the logical conditions of their identification. Not so Husserl. He starts with a different concept of relation in mind. He thinks that the concept of logical equivalence can be meaningfully analysed only after a close study of the way in which objects are constituted as objects through mental relations and mental acts. Frege's analysis is purely logical and formal. Husserl's analysis is intentional and descriptive. At this stage, Husserl's interest in mental acts still has a strong psychologistic tinge. Later he will make great efforts to remove every suggestion of psychologism from his inquiry. But the attitude he took towards the whole problem of relations will remain a decisive factor throughout his philosophical development.

3

CRITICISM OF PSYCHOLOGISM AND THE
SEARCH FOR THE PHILOSOPHICAL
PRESUPPOSITIONS OF LOGIC

In the years following the publication on *Philosophy of Arithmetic*
Husserl was led gradually to reconsider his views of the fundamental
nature of psychological analysis, and, as was pointed out earlier,
this was partly due to Frege's influence. Husserl never adopted
Frege's method of logical analysis but he was very impressed by
Frege's argument against psychologism. Psychologism is psychology
in the wrong place, and according to Frege psychology is certainly
out of place in logic. In the Preface to his *Fundamental Laws of
Arithmetic* Frege launched a strong attack against the then wide-
spread psychologistic tendencies in logic. He saw in these tendencies
one of the main barriers to the understanding of his own logicist
programme. Logic, he remarks, seems to be utterly infected by
psychology. Yet, he thinks it should be quite obvious that logical
truths, which according to him include the vast domain of mathematical truths, are not and cannot be psychological truths. They are
quite inexplicable on psychological premises. The truths of logic,
he maintains, do not depend on whether someone accepts them or
rejects them. What is logically true does not depend on any act of
evaluation or judgement. The acts of judging are empirical acts in
space and time; what is logically true is not tied to any place or
time (*das Wahrsein . . . ist ort und zeitlos*). It is, Frege thinks, absolutely necessary to make a clear distinction between what is true
in itself and our regarding something as true (*Fürwahrhalten*).
Psychology investigates the latter; the former should be the subject
of a purely logical inquiry.

The accent here is on what is 'true in itself'. Not what is true by general concensus, not what is believed to be true, not what is true only as long as we are here and agree to call it thus, but, what is true because it shows things as they really are, what is objectively true. This objective truth, as Frege sees it, cannot be explained in genetic terms and therefore psychology is out of place in logic.

In his *Logical Investigations* Husserl put forward similar views. He accepted Frege's criticism of psychologism and emphasised the need for logic to re-examine its own foundations. Logical theory was in a state of confusion. Logic had been interpreted from a variety of different aspects with the origin and the nature of logical problems becoming, if anything, more obscured. Logic had sometimes been regarded as part of psychology, sometimes the approach to logical problems was made through a psychologistically oriented epistemology, and sometimes logic was regarded as a department of metaphysics. Husserl rejected all these views. At the same time he rejected the view of logic as a purely regulative, purely 'practical' discipline, as a mere 'art of thinking'. Naturally logic has a normative function, but, maintains Husserl, its normative function can be understood only if we examine its theoretical basis. As far as logic is concerned, what there ought to be is based on what there is. Logical 'imperatives' are based on logical 'statements of fact'. Logic is first and foremost a theoretical discipline.

Husserl pleads for a 'pure logic' free from foreign admixtures, above all free from psychologism. The psychologism in logic according to Husserl is a form of sceptical relativism which is no sooner carefully considered than it shows itself to be absurd and self-defeating. Logic must not be judged by the standards applicable to empirical sciences. Logical laws (among which Husserl includes the laws of cardinal and ordinal arithmetic, and of 'pure set theory'[1]) are according to him *a priori* 'ideal laws' grounded in the *meaning* (or, as Husserl also calls it, 'essence', 'content') of concepts such as truth, proposition, object, quality, relation, connexion, law, fact etc., which, he says, are the categories of the building stones out of which science as such is made up. An infringement of these laws results in logical absurdities.[2]

The scope of Husserl's 'pure' logic

Having convinced himself of the inadequacy of a psychological analysis of mathematical and logical concepts Husserl concentrated his efforts on clarifying the structure—and the scope—of logic. He focused his attention on what he called the 'objective-logical' (distinguished by him from the 'noetic') conditions of knowledge.

[1] cf. *Logische Untersuchungen*, vol. I, p. 144.
[2] cf. ibid., p. 122.

It looked as if he was losing interest in epistemological problems. He reacted against his own 'psychologistic misconceptions' by putting emphasis on the autonomy and theoretical self-sufficiency of logic. However, his epistemological interests soon reasserted themselves and he began a systematic analysis of the noetic presuppositions of logic—his analysis, as we shall see, soon expanding into an analysis of the conditions of the possibility of knowledge in general.

But let us take a closer look at his conception of logic. What he (in the first volume of *Logical Investigations*) calls 'pure logic' has one principal aim: to explore the conditions that make theory and theoretic explanation possible; to clarify the 'essence' of theory. According to Husserl, its first task is to establish and clarify the categories of the 'building stones' of theory and science in general, some of which have already been mentioned. These categories are of two kinds. One group consists of the categories that refer to the meanings of expressions and concatenations of expressions—e.g. 'concept', 'proposition', 'truth', etc. Husserl calls them the 'pure meaning-categories'. The other group consists of the categories that refer to the objects that expressions are about or aim at, and are called by Husserl the 'pure object-categories'. They include 'object', 'state of affairs', 'plurality', 'cardinal number', 'relation', 'connexion', etc. Next, the 'pure logic' must investigate the laws grounded in these categories. An example of the laws grounded in the meaning-categories are the laws of syllogistic inference. On the side of objects, an example is provided by the theory of cardinal numbers which (according to Husserl) is grounded in the category of *cardinal number*.

The distinction between these two types of categories—they are to be understood, according to Husserl, as modifications of 'meaning in general' and 'object in general' respectively—is regarded by Husserl to be of the greatest importance and he reverted to it in his *Formal and Transcendental Logic* (1929) where he used it to explain the difference between what he called the 'apophantic logic' (logic of judgement) and the 'formal ontology'. The 'apophantic logic' and the 'formal ontology', according to him, represent the two fundamental aspects of *formal logic*. The domain of what he now called 'formal logic' coincides basically with that of 'pure logic'. The 'apophantic analysis', according to Husserl, is concerned with judgements, or rather with propositions and propositional structures. The 'formal ontology', on the other hand, is according to him 'an *a priori* science concerned with objects in general'; its 'theme' is not 'judgement' but 'object in general', 'something in general', and the concepts derived from, and related to, these. It includes, among others, theory of numbers and set-theory.

However, there is one further task that 'pure logic' (or formal logic) is called upon to perform. It must explore the various possible *forms* of theories and study the structure and the problems of construction of deductive systems. Its task besides that of clarifying the basic meaning-categories and the basic object-categories and the laws based on them must be to study the various propositional systems as theoretic wholes with a view to providing a general theory of deductive systems.

It is clear from this brief outline that Husserl takes a very wide view of 'pure' or formal logic. Formal logic, according to him, fulfils the function of a *theory of science*—not, however, a philosophical theory of science, but an *analytic* theory of science. The latter distinction is important to bear in mind if one is to understand his later 'transcendental' argument. Its meaning will become clearer as we go on expounding his views. But a hint as to what it implies gives already the distinction quoted earlier between the 'objective-logical' and the 'noetic' conditions of knowledge. Formal logic investigates the 'objective-logical' conditions of knowledge and as long as it leaves the noetic conditions out of account it can never fulfil the function of a philosophical theory of science in a proper sense.

According to Husserl, an approach towards such a philosophical theory of science could be made through an analysis of the noetic presuppositions of logic. What is needed, according to him, is a philosophy of logic—a philosophy which whilst clarifying the noetic presuppositions of logic would at the same time explain the conditions of the possibility of theoretic knowledge in general. Such a philosophy, according to Husserl, would have to take into consideration the 'subjective' as well as the 'objective' aspect of knowledge. This is the crucial point in Husserl's whole philosophical position and one that marks off his efforts from anything that Frege was contemplating. Husserl's view, in short, is that whilst it is necessary to guard against psychologism and relativism, it is equally necessary to guard against the blind *objectivism* which does not see, or refuses to see, the need for exploring the noetic presuppositions of objective truth, and in consequence is entirely unable to make philosophical sense of logic and science.

But before considering further his criticism of 'blind objectivism' let us take another look at his anti-relativist position. Husserl assumes that the basic logical laws underlying theoretical thought are all necessary truths inexplicable in psychological terms and he goes on to ask what are the conditions that make such laws and their application possible; what are the conditions that make logic and theory possible. These questions, from his point of view, lead inevitably from a formal to a *transcendental logic*, i.e. into the field

of a transcendental philosophy. We shall see later how he proposed
to develop such a transcendental philosophy.

But, one might ask, on what grounds do we decide that the logical
laws are without exception 'necessary truths'? Might it not be that
Husserl starts with wrong premises? It has been argued by many
logicians that no *intrinsic* necessity attaches to any logical 'axiom'
and that the value of such axioms should be judged exclusively in
relation to what can actually be accomplished with their help. The
view that has gained considerable acceptance in recent times is
that the so-called logical 'axioms' should be treated as postulates
and definitions; their status is occasionally compared with the
status of the 'axioms' of the various systems of geometry. Much of
Frege's and Husserl's criticism against psychologism has ceased to
be relevant in the conditions now prevailing in logic. Today few
logicians would deserve to be labelled 'psychologists', but a considerable number of them would opt for some form of conventionalism. It is the conventionalist rather than the psychologistic
arguments that Husserl would have to meet.

The controversy over the status of logical principles

The situation in logic, and especially in set-theory—as a critic of
Husserl might very well point out—has changed profoundly since
the beginning of the century. Both Frege and Husserl held the view
(at least before 1901) that all logical laws, including the set-theoretical
laws, were equally 'apodictic'. But ever since Russell discovered
his famous paradox[1] in 1901, set-theory has been in a state of
ferment and conventionalism has been steadily gaining ground.
We now have a choice of different set-theoretical systems and the
claims to uniqueness and apodicticity have largely been abandoned.

The trend towards conventionalism and 'contextualism' which
has become the dominant trend in set-theory has tended to spread
to elementary logic as well. For—it is asked—what guarantees the
universal validity and necessity of elementary logic and its laws?
What justification is there for regarding elementary logic as an
'oasis of certainty' with laws immune to change? The doubts underlying these questions concern the concept of analyticity. It used to

---

[1] The paradox is about classes that are not members of themselves. A class is
normally not a member of itself. The class of chairs is not itself a chair. If we now
form a class of all classes that are not members of themselves will this class be a
member of itself or will it not be a member of itself? Either assumption leads to a
contradiction. This paradox made it necessary to introduce various restrictions
into set-theory (or theory of classes) so as to exclude the predicates that give rise
to contradictions. However, these restrictions have themselves often caused new
difficulties and the gains in consistency have been made only at the expense of
completeness.

be thought that the certainty of elementary logic was firmly rooted in its analyticity, its laws containing the evidence of their own truth. But the principle of analyticity has come to grief in set-theory and this has raised doubts about the whole concept of analyticity and about the status of logical laws generally. It was Frege who tried to derive mathematics from a set of analytic logical principles. But his attempt ended in failure. Among the basic laws which formed the foundations of his logical system of arithmetic there was one concerning value-ranges, or extensions of concepts, which was subsequently shown to lead to contradictions. This was the famous axiom (V) from his *Fundamental Laws of Arithmetic* whose vulnerability was exposed by Russell's paradox. With this one important section of what Husserl called 'pure' logic was shown to be non-analytic and therefore susceptible to conventionalist interpretations.

The discovery of Russell's paradox had far-reaching repercussions in mathematical logic. Frege's logico-mathematical programme was recognised as inadequate. Russell's attempt to revive it in a somewhat revised form was far from being an unqualified success. Russell found that he had to strengthen his logical premisses with certain additional non-analytical postulates in order to make his own logicist programme work, and this made many people wonder whether all logical 'laws' should not be regarded as *postulates* and treated accordingly. Today many logicians speak of different 'logics' rather than of 'logic' in the singular. The result of the intervention of logic in mathematics seems thus to have been not only the discovery of the limitations of elementary logic but also a certain erosion of its basic structure. An important factor in this process has been the controversy around the problem of infinity and, in connexion with this, the abandonment by many mathematicians of the principle of Excluded Middle.

This was not how Husserl looked at logic. He (at least at the time when he wrote his *Logical Investigations*) would have dismissed as incoherent the idea of a logic in which the principle that every proposition is either true or false is not valid. From his point of view, the abandonment of any logical principle would amount to asserting that the concept of truth means something different from what it really does mean. Logical relativism, in his view, leads to absurdities. Writing about the principle of Non-contradiction and the principle of Excluded Middle, he says: 'If the relativist says that there could be beings not bound by these principles ... he means either that these beings could express in their judgements propositions and truths which do not conform to these principles or that their judging psychologically does not proceed in accordance with these principles. As far as the latter is concerned, there is nothing surpris-

ing about this for we ourselves are such beings. . . . As for the
former, our answer would be simply this: either those beings understand the words true and false in the sense in which we understand
them—in which case it is silly to say that these principles are not
valid for they belong to the very meaning of these words, in the
sense in which we understand the latter. . . . Or, they use the words
true and false in a different sense in which case the whole quarrel
is a quarrel about words.'[1]

Husserl implies here that the 'sense in which we understand these
words' is the correct sense; but the question is, who is 'we', and why
should it be assumed that there is just one sense in which these words
can appropriately be used? In particular, why should it be assumed
that the principles of Excluded Middle must belong to the meaning
of these words? This would imply that unless we recognised the
principle we could not claim to have understood the meaning of
truth correctly, but this is a metaphysical assumption which requires
justification. The principle says that every proposition is either true
or false, but it seems clear that many propositions are neither.
The proposition 'The gods do not think logically' is neither true
nor false; to assume otherwise would mean accepting that there
are gods. With some propositions, such as those in works of fiction,
the question of truth or falsehood does not even arise, while with
many others it is impossible to devise a method of verification which
would enable us to come to a definite decision as to their truth-value.
Propositions about infinite numbers belong in the latter category,
and to maintain, in spite of the impossibility of verification, that
such propositions must be either true or false would mean making
a metaphysical assertion for which there can be no adequate justification in purely mathematical terms.

It is clear that powerful objections can be raised against the
principle of Excluded Middle and that this principle cannot be
applied to propositions in an unrestricted sense. But if this is so,
one may wonder what justification there is for regarding the principle
as absolutely indispensable and as belonging to the 'meaning of
truth' in the sense in which Husserl uses this phrase.

The criticism directed against the principle of Excluded Middle
is often widened to include all other basic principles of traditional
elementary logic. What is attacked is the assumption of their
universal validity and necessity. For, it is asked, what does it mean
to say that the logical principles, even if carefully restricted to the
least vulnerable ones such as e.g. the principle of Non-contradiction
or *modus ponens*, are universally valid, or, in the often used Leib-
nizian phrase, true in 'all possible worlds'? If a 'possible world'

[1] *Logische Untersuchungen*, vol. I, p. 118.

can be identified only on the basis of its conformity with these principles then by saying that these principles hold for 'all possible worlds' we assert no more than that they apply to whatever conforms to them. The phrase 'true in all possible worlds', it is said, reflects the tendency to give to these laws an ontological interpretation, to regard them as 'ontological invariants', whereas the simple truth is that they are employed as stipulations or postulates which define what we understand by the consistency of discourse.[1] This being the case there is no justification for giving them an ontological status.

However, this criticism begs many questions. For (just as in Husserl's quotation earlier) it is not made clear who precisely is meant by 'we'. It is equally obscure what 'stipulations and postulates' means in this context. Surely, we cannot say that the law of Non-contradiction is a result of deliberate choice. But if we cannot but accept it as true in what sense is it stipulated? It would lead us too far to go into this argument in any detail. It is clear however that the conflict about the status and the function of the basic logical principles raises much wider issues. What is at stake is the whole concept of objective truth.

The objectivity of truth and the subjectivity of the 'act of knowledge'

Frege, we saw earlier, was anxious to make a distinction between what is true in itself or just true, and someone's regarding something as true. The most objectionable feature of psychologism as well as of other forms of logical relativism from his standpoint was that they blurred this distinction, and in doing so they blurred the distinction between *beliefs* and *facts*. Husserl agreed. So, incidentally, did Russell. They all shared the view that logic is based on a concept of truth that cannot be explained in terms of what is acceptable, or not acceptable, to us or to any particular section of the human race. It is based on the concept of objective truth and objective truth presupposes an objective reality of facts. Logical relativism with its doctrine of the relativity of truth, they all seem to agree, implies that there is no such reality; that there is no fundamental difference between a believed-in world and a world of facts. This is why it must be 'resisted'.

Russell's own position is especially interesting in this connexion. Whilst criticising the traditional logic for its many inadequacies and introducing many changes and innovations to free logic from undesirable ontological influences—and thereby, in effect, laying the foundations for an ontology-free logic—he nevertheless accepted the general thesis about the connexion between logical truth and an

[1] See Ernest Nagel, 'Logic without Ontology', in *Philosophy of Mathematics, selected readings*, Ed. H. Putnam and P. Benaceraf (New Jersey, 1964), p. 308.

objective reality. He was out of sympathy with the relativistic trends in logic and he showed this by his determined defence of the principle of Excluded Middle. As we saw earlier, the principle was criticised, among others, on the grounds that it is inapplicable, or rather that it cannot be shown to be applicable, to the cases where there is no method available for verifying either of the given alternatives. Russell's reply to this criticism is that it confuses truth with verifiability. What is true, maintains Russell, need *not* necessarily be verifiable. If a person is found dead with a gun at his side those investigating his death act on the assumption that he either committed suicide or did not commit suicide, and feel justifiably certain that one of the alternatives must be true, although they may never be able to discover which.

Russell defends this principle (or 'law', as he prefers to call it) because from his standpoint it represents a clear link between logic and the objective reality of facts. He insists on this link and on the necessity of a distinction between what is true and what is held to be true—a distinction which Frege used so successfully in his attack on psychologism.

Husserl shares this view. He entirely agrees with Frege and Russell as far as the objectivity of truth is concerned. What he does not like is their 'objectivism', i.e. their failure to take adequately into account the subjective aspect of knowledge. The subjective aspect of knowledge is just as important, and the main problem, as Husserl sees it, is one of reconciling the objectivity of truth with the subjectivity of the act of knowledge. The questions he asks and tries to answer are: 'How are we to understand the fact that the "in itself" of the objectivity can be thought of by us and moreover "apprehended" in cognition and thus in the end yet become "subjective"; what does it mean that the object exists "in itself" and is at the same time "given" in knowledge; how does the ideality of the general expressed in a concept or a law enter the stream of real mental experiences and become part of the knowledge of the thinking subject; what does the cognitive *adequatio rei ac intellectus* mean in the various cases, according as the cognitive apprehension is directed to an individual object or something general, a fact or a law, etc.'[1] These are the problems that interest Husserl.

Formal logic is concerned with the 'objective-logical' conditions of knowledge. But the 'noetic conditions' too must be explored. There is a host of problems that fall outside the scope of formal logic and, according to Husserl, these problems can be clarified only through a *phenomenological analysis* of knowledge. We need a phenomenological analysis of knowledge in order to be able to

[1] *Logische Untersuchungen,* vol II, p. 8.

make sense of logic and to explain its various presuppositions. Such an analysis however, leads us, according to Husserl, into the domain of a *subjectivity* of which formal logic knows nothing.

The concept of an object-constituting
subjectivity—die leistende Subjektivität

The central concept in Husserl's phenomenological analysis of knowledge is that of an active, meaning-giving, object-constituting subjectivity—*die leistende Subjektivität*. The term 'Leistung' which Husserl often uses and which is difficult to translate means that which is accomplished in an intentional act or a series of such acts. The subjectivity of which he speaks, it should be pointed out at once, is not a 'psychological subjectivity', it is not the mental events as studied by psychology; he is not interested in what is psychologically accomplished by any one person or a group of persons, but in the accomplishment of the subjectivity as such. The concept of subjectivity in his earliest phenomenological investigations coincides with that of intentional acts; later, as we shall see, he interpreted this subjectivity in a wider sense as the subjectivity of a 'transcendental Ego'.

But more about this later. The important thing to bear in mind is that this meaning-giving, object-constituting subjectivity represents an area which, according to Husserl, must be thoroughly explored if we want to clarify the presuppositions of logic and provide a true philosophical theory of science. We cannot do this as long as we persist in the attitude of a 'blind objectivism'. What logic stands in need of, according to Husserl, is a thoroughgoing philosophical *self-criticism*. Such a self-criticism, according to him, will show that logical concepts and logical schemata are not just items to be analysed and defined in terms of other items of similar nature but are the product of a *categorial activity* which must be phenomenologically explored. What logicians usually overlook, or simply ignore, according to Husserl, is this activity; they speak of categories, but they forget the categorial activity without which there would be no categories.

The point that Husserl wants to make is, briefly, this: A purely conceptual analysis is not enough, it is not enough to study the structure of theories and categorial frameworks, to analyse the technical problems of construction of scientific systems and the logical structure of the scientific argument—all this, useful and necessary though it is, is not enough to enable us to understand fully the meaning of science. We must clarify the nature and the sources of the *activity* which lies behind all this and which the theoretician takes for granted. 'We must'—says Husserl—'rise above the self-obliviousness of the theoretician who while preoccupied with things, theories and methods is quite unaware of the interiority of his productive thought (*die Innerlichkeit seines Leistens*) and who while living in these things, theories, methods, never focuses his attention on his own productive activity.'[1]

We must, in other words, make the *leistende Subjektivität* the object of our inquiry. In insisting that we should turn our attention to our own productive mental activity Husserl makes a decisive step away from Frege and reaffirms, though in a modified form, some of the basic ideas that guided his analysis in his *Philosophy of Arithmetic*. He has renounced psychologism but has not abandoned his interest in the 'subjective' conditions of knowledge. It was this interest that originally led him to concern himself with intentional relations and since intentionality remained the main theme of his analyses we must now examine this concept in more detail.

[1] *Formale und Transzendentale Logik,* 1929, p. 14.

4

INTENTIONALITY

First, a brief terminological explanation. The word 'intentional'—as is clear from what was said earlier about intentional relations—is a technical term and must not be confused with its counterpart in ordinary language, although obviously there is a vestige of etymological meaning common to both. In ordinary language the words 'intend', 'intention' and their derivatives have a variety of uses. Most frequently they are used to communicate something about our or other people's actions or attitudes. Sometimes their function is merely to convey what our or somebody else's action will be. At other times, they serve to emphasise the determination of the speaker to carry out what he has resolved to do. Further, we speak of someone having done something 'intentionally' when we want to say that what he did he did deliberately and consciously. On other occasions, 'intention' may refer simply to what is meant. When a speaker, anxious not to be mistaken, explains what he 'had in mind' when he used certain words or phrases, he tries to make clear what he *intended* to say. If there is something that accompanies the use of these words in all these different cases then it is an experience of aiming, of attending to something in some special way. It is with regard to this feature that 'intention' and 'intentional' can be interpreted as descriptive of all mental acts in which we direct ourselves to something in some way or other; as descriptive of experiences (intellectual or emotional) in which we stand in a *relation to an object*.

It was Franz Brentano who was essentially responsible for introducing this conception of intentionality into modern philosophy.

Brentano was trying to clarify the distinction between physical and mental phenomena and he thought that one of the main differences between the two types of phenomena is to be found in the fact that mental phenomena unlike physical ones are characterised by so-called 'intentional inexistence' (of the intended object), or, more simply, by intentional relations. It is best to quote his own explanation from his *Psychology from the Empirical Standpoint*: 'Every mental phenomenon'—he says—'is characterised by what the Schoolmen of the Middle Ages called the intentional (also mental) inexistence of an object, and what we could call—although using not quite unambiguous words—relation to a content, direction upon an object (which is not here to be taken as something real) or immanent objectivity. Every such phenomenon contains within itself something as an object, although not all contain objects in the same way. In a presentation (*Vorstellung*) something is presented, in a judgement something is affirmed or denied, in love something is loved, in hate something is hated, in desire something is desired, etc.'[1]

The 'intentional inexistence of an object' is here given as a main characteristic of mental phenomena. The words 'inexistence' and 'immanent objectivity' are a reminder not to confuse the existence of intentional objects with extra-mental reality. The objects of presentation, desire, love, hate, etc., may, but need not, exist extra-mentally. From the fact that someone thinks about God, loves God, hates God, desires God nothing can be inferred about God's actual existence. But while in certain cases no inferences can be made about extra-mental reality from otherwise true propositions, in certain other cases such inferences seem quite legitimate. Thus, for example, if 'Jones has just picked up a book from the shelf and is holding it in his hands' is true then it follows that there is indeed something such that Jones has picked it up and is holding it in his hands. We could not, unless we are using the words 'to pick up' and 'to hold' in some obscure metaphorical sense, accept the one and reject the other.

This has caused some logicians in more recent times to draw a distinction between 'intentional' and 'non-intentional' verbs and to concentrate on the analysis of the logical consequences that the use of one or the other of these two types of verbs has in various contexts. Thus 'to think' (about something), 'to desire' (something), 'to look for' (something), etc., are described as 'intentional' because they do not require the existence of their objects. 'To love' and 'to hate' are regarded with some doubt for these verbs seem to allow of both

[1] F. Brentano, *Psychologie vom empirischen Standpunkt* (Leipzig, Felix Meier, 1924), vol. I, p. 124.

intentional and non-intentional uses. 'To perceive', on the other hand, is generally described as non-intentional. One cannot *perceive* something, it is said, without there actually being something for one to perceive. 'To believe' is regarded as intentional on account of the fact that it is quite possible to believe a false proposition. 'To know', on the other hand, is regarded as non-intentional; for it is said, whilst Jones may very well believe that the earth is flat, he cannot *know* this, for one cannot know a falsehood.

However, it must be pointed out that Brentano himself did not regard the intentional relation as a property of verbs but as a *mental relation*. This relation involves a mental act, and while it does not imply the extra-mental existence of the object of such an act, it does presuppose the existence of a *subject*, that is, of someone who believes, hates, loves, etc. It is with the idea of a subject in mind that Brentano spoke at first of 'inexistence' and 'mental inexistence' of intentional objects, although he later regarded these terms as somewhat misleading and laid the main emphasis on what he called 'relation to an object' (*Beziehung auf ein Objekt*).

The point to remember is that this 'relation to an object', the intentional relation, was from the very beginning associated with *mental acts*. It was seen by both Brentano and Husserl as an expression of 'mental activity' (although Husserl in trying to prevent psychologistic misconceptions generally preferred the term 'intentional' to 'mental'). The study of the linguistic aspects of intentionality is both necessary and important, but one could argue—and our two philosophers would have argued—that the phenomenological (or, as Brentano would rather have said 'psychognostic') aspects must be analysed first if we are to get to the heart of the problem. We cannot gain an understanding of the activity of the mind without examining this activity from the 'inside'.

Mental acts and consciousness

Another characteristic of mental phenomena, according to Brentano, is that they are perceived only in 'inner consciousness', that is to say that they are objects of 'inner perception' (*innere Wahrnehmung*). Since they alone are given in 'inner perception', says Brentano, they alone are given as directly evident. The concept of the evident plays an important role in both Brentano and Husserl's philosophies. But why does Brentano think that mental phenomena are perceived only in 'inner consciousness'? The reason for this becomes clear if we look at some of the examples he gave of physical and mental phenomena. A colour, a tone, a musical chord, a figure, are to Brentano physical phenomena, but *seeing* a coloured figure or *hearing* a musical chord are not. Seeing something or hearing something must be distinguished from the objects we see or hear. Similarly, knowing something, disbelieving something, enjoying something must be distinguished from what we know, disbelieve, enjoy. An emotion, an expectation, a doubt, a belief—they all, according to Brentano, belong to mental phenomena. What he has in mind are of course the *acts* of expecting, doubting, imagining, believing, etc. All these acts are intentional acts directed upon some object. When Brentano speaks of a mental phenomenon he has in mind some kind of act-object relation; not a relation in the ordinary sense, not a relation between two otherwise independent terms but what later phenomenologists called the 'relation of consciousness'. And he distinguishes various classes of mental phenomena according to the character of different acts.

However, the concept of consciousness requires here further clarification. Mental phenomena are said to be 'conscious' phenomena. Every mental act, Brentano points out, is a conscious act. But what precisely is involved in such a conscious experience? Is the consciousness that we have of a mental phenomenon something beyond and above this phenomenon or is it something that is in principle indistinguishable from it? The critics of consciousness point out that the assumption of the existence of certain separate 'acts of consciousness' would inevitably lead to a multiplicity of acts and an infinite regress. Suppose someone strikes a note on the piano in the room next door and the sound is sufficiently loud to draw my attention. In this case two things at least will have to be distinguished: first, the sound which reached my ear, and, secondly, my hearing it—the latter being (according to Brentano) a mental phenomenon in which I have the sound as an object. I hear a sound coming from the room next door and I am at the same time conscious of my hearing it. If now this consciousness is an act distinguishable from the act of hearing itself then there seems *prima facie* no reason why there should not be a third order act, a fourth order act, etc., each directed upon its predecessor and becoming in turn the object of an act of a higher order. Which would result in a consciousness of consciousness of consciousness, and so on *ad infinitum.*

Brentano denies that there is a danger of such a regress. First of all, my having something as an object—in our example, the sound coming from the room next door—and my consciousness of having something as an object are parts of *one and the same* mental phenomenon. It is of course possible, and indeed necessary, to make a clear distinction between the sound and the hearing of the sound—and Brentano refers to them as the 'primary' and the 'secondary object' respectively. But he points out at the same time that the 'secondary object' of an act cannot be observed in the way in which its 'primary object' is observed. The consciousness of a conscious act is transparent, in the sense that it includes self-consciousness as a constituent part.

Consequently, there is no multiplicity of acts and no infinite regress. There are—according to Brentano—only different *ways* in which we may be conscious of having something as an object. This depends on whether the given object is merely an object of a presentation (*Vorstellung*), or whether it is an object of a judgement, or whether it is an object of an emotion. In accordance with this, Brentano distinguishes between *three* classes of mental phenomena and refers to them under the headings of 'presentation', 'judgement' and 'the phenomena of love and hate', respectively. To return to our example, I may contemplate the sound that I hear merely as an object of presentation, or I may make it the object of a cognitive act as expressed in a judgement, or I may feel pleased or displeased at hearing it.

But all this is a good deal more complicated than might at first appear. First of all, all these different acts involve a distinction between 'primary' and 'secondary' objects. In other words, they—in a sense—combine consciousness with self-consciousness. To quote Brentano: 'Every act, even the simplest, has therefore a twofold object—a primary and a secondary one. The simplest act, such as e.g. the act in which we hear something, has a tone as its primary object, and it has itself, that is, the mental phenomenon in which the tone is heard, as a secondary object.'[1] Once we have accepted the interpretation of mental phenomena in terms of mental acts, some distinction of this kind seems indeed to be inevitable, especially if we want to avoid the regress mentioned earlier. But this does not necessarily make the reflective consciousness of mental acts easier to understand. Nor is it very clear precisely what status the 'primary objects' have. For if these objects are given to us only intentionally, that is, in mental acts, how do we decide whether such an object is real or merely imaginary? Another problem concerns the so-called 'unity of consciousness'. We saw that there are different kinds of acts and, consequently, different ways of being conscious of having something as an object. How do these different acts combine to produce the 'unity of consciousness' without which our mental life would disintegrate? We might try to explain this phenomenon in casual terms. But this would lead us into the field of 'physical phenomena' and it is maintained that there is a fundamental difference between these phenomena and 'mental phenomena'. These were some of the problems which Brentano faced and it cannot be said

[1] ibid., p. 218.

that he found an entirely satisfactory solution to any of them, although his analysis represents undoubtedly a major contribution towards their clarification.

The striking thing about Brentano's analysis is its many distinctly Cartesian features; in particular, his classification of mental phenomena can be traced back to Descartes. It is significant that the preoccupation with intentionality which his analysis inspired aroused a new and profound interest in the Cartesian *cogito* and 'Cartesian subjectivity'. Phenomenology has a Cartesian ancestry even though it repudiates the Cartesian metaphysics.

Husserl's objections to Brentano

The phenomenon of intentionality, as Brentano's analysis indicates, is inseparable from the phenomenon of *consciousness*. In the 'phenomenological school' great emphasis is laid on what is called the 'intentionality of consciousness', the 'intentional nature of consciousness', and there are phenomenologists who regard a phenomenological analysis of consciousness as the most fundamental philosophical task. But Brentano's own analysis is widely rejected as psychologistic and as philosophically altogether inadequate.

The main critic of Brentano's 'psychologism' was Husserl himself. Having begun his philosophical career from a distinctly Brentanian position he became convinced as a result of his continued preoccupation with logic and the problem of meaning that the 'objective' element in knowledge cannot be explained from psychologistic premises. Although we must take into account the 'subjective' aspect of knowledge, although we need a concept of subjectivity, this subjectivity, maintains Husserl, cannot be a psychologistically conceived subjectivity.

Unlike Brentano, Husserl was not interested in a classification of mental phenomena, or in defining the field of psychology. He was interested primarily to find out in what way intentionality could help towards an explanation of the 'noetic' conditions of objective truth. He did not speak of 'mental phenomena' but of 'intentional experiences', of acts taken not in a psychological but in a purely phenomenological sense. In his discussion of intentional relations he points out that it is highly misleading to speak of an intentional experience 'containing something within itself as an object'. This might suggest a real, material sort of relation between a consciousness (or an 'ego') and an object of this consciousness, whereas nothing of the kind is the case. Or it might suggest that the act and the intentional object are equally to be found as something real within consciousness, which would also be a grave misconception. The intentional object is not an image or an idea within a (psychological, empirical) consciousness. Nor is it necessarily a transcendent physical thing. It is what is intended in the act, no more and no less. When I think of 'my favourite novel' the object of my thought is not the picture that I have in my mind of the book that I like reading; nor is it the actual copy of the book that I possess. It is not a physical object at all. It belongs to an entirely different category. Intentional objects must not be confused with mental objects or physical objects. They are simply objects of certain signifying intentions.

Husserl consequently rejects the term 'mental inexistence' (which Brentano himself subsequently discarded). In short, he wants to eliminate all 'psychological misconceptions' and use a phenomenologically purified concept of intentionality in his analysis of meaning.

His campaign against psychologism led him in the end to adopt a radically anti-empiricist transcendentalist position with the result that the concept of intentionality too received a transcendental interpretation and acquired a much wider philosophical significance. He eventually introduced concepts such as 'transcendental consciousness', 'transcendental subjectivity' and 'transcendental Ego' into his philosophy. The distaste for relativism of any kind, the wish to remove every suggestion of psychologism from his theory of intentional acts and the intense preoccupation with the *'a priori* conditions of the possibility of objective knowledge' led him to revise his earlier 'descriptively psychological' approach in favour of a transcendental view. He moved closer to Kant. We shall see later that he worked out a special method which, he hoped, would enable him to develop phenomenology as a pure 'transcendental science'.

However, his adoption of the transcendental viewpoint, in a sense, was only a final step in his effort to reconcile the objectivity of knowledge with the 'subjective conditions' of knowing, and we shall be in a better position to judge the significance of this step if we examine more closely his earlier views, especially the role that intentional acts play in his analysis of meaning. A few preliminary explanations about the distinctions he draws between signs and expressions and between meaning-giving and meaning-fulfilling acts will facilitate an understanding of what is to follow.

Signs, expressions and acts

Every sign, Husserl says, is a sign of something, but not every sign has a meaning, a sense which is expressed with the help of a sign.[1] The word 'sign', he points out, is often used ambiguously: in the sense of a mark or sign indicative of something (*Anzeige*) and in the sense of an expression (*Ausdruck*). It is of the utmost importance to distinguish between these two things clearly. A sign in the sense of a

[1] *Logische Untersuchungen*, vol. II/1, p. 23.

'mark' only points to the object or the state of affairs of which it is a sign; it does not 'express' anything beyond this. Expressions, on the other hand, involve intentional acts and have an altogether different status. They are part of *language*. Expressions are signs 'animated by meaning'. They refer to something solely in virtue of what they mean.

In the case of marks we have a simple relation of indication between a sign and the object indicated by the sign. The link between the two may be established by an arbitrary convention, or it may be based on a causal, contextual or some other connexion that exists between them. Many road signs, for example, function as stipulated indicatory signs. An example of non-stipulated signs are the symptoms that a medical expert recognises as indicative of a developing disease. The referring function of an indicatory sign or 'mark' is understood as the result of an association of ideas, and a link by association, as is well known, can be forged at a very low level of mental development. Conditioned reflexes can form a basis of such associative links. But irrespective of the way in which marks come to mark something they all have one thing in common: they are all objects indicating the presence or suggesting the existence of some other objects or states of affairs.

Expressions, on the other hand—according to Husserl—belong in the domain of spoken or written language. They are linguistic, but they are not to be understood as signs in what it has recently become fashionable to call a 'language-game'. Their function is to transmit certain meanings and to serve as vehicles of communication. In communication they draw attention to certain 'meaning-giving' acts of their users. But they do not have to be actually used in communication in order to be meaningful. We can talk to other people but we can also 'talk to ourselves'. It is intentional acts that are important. It is these acts that ultimately hold the key to the difference between expressions and marks.

At this point, the relevance of what has been said earlier about subjectivity and consciousness becomes apparent. For Husserl's analysis clearly implies that a distinction between signs as marks and signs as expressions, as he understands it, can be drawn only from the standpoint of the subjectively evident. From an *external* standpoint there are no acts and, consequently, the distinction is less easy to justify. Externally, expressions may be interpreted as complex signs indicative of certain situations, objects, contextual relationships, behavioural patterns, etc. But, if this is so then the above distinction so far from vindicating an introduction of intentional acts into logical discourse presupposes in fact an acceptance of such acts.

However, Husserl believes that an 'external' (or behaviourist) approach to the problem of meaning is inadequate and he thinks that its limitations justify the introduction of acts. One of Husserl's main objections against the 'external' approach is that it makes it impossible for us to grasp certain relations of analytic and non-analytic necessity between expressions. The fact that '*A* is an equiangular triangle' *necessarily implies* '*A* is an equilateral triangle' or that '*A* is blue all over' *necessarily excludes* '*A* is red all over' cannot, in Husserl's view, be explained by means of any external empirical analysis. The truth of what is here said is grounded in the meanings of the expressions used and can be understood only after these meanings and their mutual relationships have been understood. We must be able to direct our attention in phenomenological reflection to meanings as ideal objects and, for this, he points out, we need acts.

However, not only reflecting on an expression, but also using an expression, according to Husserl, involves an act. It is important in this connexion to explain Husserl's distinction between meaning-*giving* and meaning-*fulfilling* acts. According to Husserl, an expression comes to life, begins to mean something, as a result of a meaning-giving act. But many expressions thus animated by meaning-giving acts do not refer to actually existing or even possible objects. This is why a meaning-giving act, according to Husserl, may result in a 'disappointment', it may remain cognitively unfulfilled. A meaning-intention may fail to 'find' its object. It may or may not be capable of fulfilment or it may be fulfilled only partially and inadequately. If fulfilment is to be possible we need some kind of perceptual or conceptual 'illustration'. An act of fulfilment, in a sense, provides evidence of a meaning-intention succeeding in its *reference*. The nature of fulfilment, inevitably, will depend on whether the object aimed at in a meaning-intention is an empirical particular, a universal or a state of affairs. Consequently, there will be different kinds of 'intuitive acts'.

Husserl is here, of course, merely reformulating in the phenomenological language of acts the old and familiar distinction between the conceptual and the perceptual aspect of knowledge. Knowledge, as philosophers are constantly reminding us, consists neither in concepts alone nor in perceptions alone but in a combination of the two. Or, in Kant's famous phrase, concepts without perceptions are empty and perceptions without concepts are blind. From Husserl's point of view however, talk of 'concepts' and 'perceptions' tends to obscure the fact that here we have to do with cognitive acts, that concepts are *thought* and objects *seen* and that adequate knowledge is an experience which must be phenomenologically investigated. Husserl

believes that his distinction between meaning-giving acts or signifying intentions and acts of fulfilment makes a more adequate explanation of the whole phenomenon of cognition possible.

Furthermore, his distinction, he thinks, gives him more flexibility
in interpreting and clarifying the two aspects of knowledge. The
'perceptual aspect' of knowledge is usually identified with sense
perception. This Husserl does not accept. He distinguishes between
the 'sense intuition' which, according to him, gives us 'sense objects'
and the 'categorial intuition' which, he says, gives us 'categorial
objects', objects of a 'higher order'. An example of an object of the
latter kind would be a state of affairs, such as the *cat's now being
on the mat*. The act of 'categorial intuition' in which this is seen to
be the case is a synthetic act which presupposes certain other acts
of identification, such as the identification of the cat as a cat and the
mat as a mat. But, according to Husserl, there are other categorial
acts which are not synthetic in this sense—acts in which we apprehend the so-called 'general objects' (universals) directly; in such an
act we not only 'mean' something general but we *perceive* it, as it
were; we apprehend the 'general object' itself. This latter case
raises special problems and we shall discuss it in more detail in the
next chapter. This will at the same time give us an opportunity to
see Husserl's phenomenological analysis in action.

5

THE PROBLEM OF GENERALITY

Husserl's doctrine of 'general objects' must be considered in the context of his criticism of empiricist nominalism. He rejects the view that the meaning of terms such as 'man', 'red' (as a noun), 'triangle', etc., can be explained in terms of the empirical particulars to which they can be truly applied. At the same time he is critical of platonism. Species, attributes, etc.—according to him—are not reducible to empirical particulars, but they are also not to be conceived as ideal archetypes existing *per se* as Platonic Ideas; nor, for that matter, can these 'general objects' be explained psychologically as 'mental constructs'. His argument is complex and often very difficult to follow. The most intelligible and—not surprisingly perhaps—the most plausible part of it is the criticism that he directs against nominalism.

Husserl invites us to focus our attention on the 'intentional content of logical experiences'. Generality, as he sees it, is a mode of meaning and there are different such modes. Consider the following propositions:

> Socrates is a man.
> All men are featherless bipeds.
> Man is a rational animal.

In the first proposition we attribute a property to an individual, in the second we say something about all members of a class of individuals, in the third we predicate something of a species as a *species*. The expressions 'a man', 'all men' and 'Man' represent here three different forms of generality which must be clearly distinguished from each other. In the first proposition the general term 'man' is used in a predicatively; it becomes part of a predicate and the generality in this case consists in the possibility of attaching the same predicate to different subjects and obtaining true propositions as a result ('Plato is a man'; 'Aristotle is a man', etc.). In the second proposition we refer to all men and the meaning of 'all men' cannot be explained simply as 'this man and that man, and . . . etc.' When we say 'all' we do not think of the members of a class individually, but we think of them collectively. However, it is the third case—exemplified by our last proposition—that is from Husserl's standpoint especially interesting. Here the subject of predication is the species *qua* species. We encounter here a new object—a 'general object'—which cannot be 'explained away' by a paraphrase of the relevant propositions. We cannot, for example, translate 'Man is a rational animal' into 'All men are rational animals' without changing the meaning of the original proposition. 'All men' and 'Man', from Husserl's standpoint, exemplify two different kinds of generality; they are not only grammatically, but logically different.

All this, according to Husserl, nominalism is unable to explain. Nominalism relies on the first kind of generality, namely the generality of concepts in their predicative function, but in so far as it couches its explanations in psychological terms it fails to give a satisfactory account of this type of generality either. However, nominalism breaks down completely in the case of *specific* generality. According to Husserl, only a phenomenological analysis of acts of meaning can help us here to find an answer to the problem.

Husserl's main emphasis is on acts of meaning and his main thesis is that the act in which we mean a general object—a species, an attribute—is of a fundamentally *different* kind from the act in which we mean an individual object, although a general object can be 'apprehended' as an object just as directly as an individual object. An analysis of meaning, according to Husserl, cannot get very far if it fails to acknowledge this vital fact. He defends his phenomenological approach by criticising the empiricist theories of abstraction and we shall understand his own views better if we examine his criticism of some of these theories.

The old controversy over 'abstract ideas'
It is necessary, first, to say something about the problem of the so-called 'abstract ideas' which was one of the main sources of controversy in Classical British Empiricism and which in various forms continues to exercise philosophical minds. The source of difficulties and puzzles is the generality of general terms. If we assume that sense experience is the only source of knowledge we

must somehow find a way of showing that meanings of general terms can be explained ultimately in terms of sense experience. But how are we to do this? How can we explain the general in terms of classes of particular objects or occurrences? Can the meaning of a general term be explained in terms of the objects to which it can be truly applied? A general term need not refer to anything; it may be an empty concept, in which case a 'referential analysis' will not be possible. Think, for example, of the word 'centaur'. But even in the case of non-empty general terms it does not seem possible to give a satisfactory referential analysis of their meaning. For one thing, a general term is not just a name designating a finite set of concrete objects or a finite set of experiences of such objects. It applies to anything that possesses the given property. Take, for example, the word 'triangle'. This word contains no reference to any particular triangle or class of triangles. The word designates all triangles, or perhaps we should say any object that is a triangle. But *how* do we understand its meaning? This was the problem which exercised Locke.

The answer he gave to this problem did not carry much conviction. We must be able, he claimed, to form an abstract idea of a triangle from the ideas that we have of concrete triangles. Such an abstract idea would include all the essential features characteristic of a triangle but would not itself correspond to any *particular* triangle. Ideas of this kind, Locke concedes, are indeed mere 'fictions and contrivances of the mind' but, he points out, they are important all the same because they facilitate communication and help us to enlarge our knowledge. Not surprisingly, he was unable to say anything more about the nature of these ideas, and Berkeley, and later Hume, subjected his views to sharp criticism. For how could anyone imagine a triangle which would not have the properties of any particular triangle—which would not in fact be a triangle at all, and would yet, miraculously, preserve all the characteristics of triangularity? To maintain that there are abstract general ideas is to maintain that we are able to imagine something which almost by definition cannot be imagined—a sheer absurdity. Berkeley regards Locke's view as quite preposterous, but he realises that we must be able to explain generality in some way, and he proposes the following solution. All ideas that we have, he says, are of necessity *concrete* ideas, but we can reach generality by taking one such concrete idea and regarding it as a *representative* of its class. 'To make this plain by an example, suppose a geometrician is demonstrating the method of cutting a line in two equal parts. He draws, for instance, a black line of an inch in length; this, which in itself is a particular line, is nevertheless with regard to its signification general, since, as it is there used, it represents all particular lines whatsoever; so that what is demonstrated of it, is demonstrated of all lines, or, in other words, of a line in general. And as that particular line becomes general, by being made a sign, so the name *line*, which taken absolutely is *particular*, by being a sign is made *general*.'[1]

Hume, for his part, points out the importance of the role of language and the inherent generality of words. He fully accepts Berkeley's criticism of Locke's 'abstract ideas'. According to Hume, ideas that we have are originally all drawn from the 'impressions' that things make upon us. Ideas are only 'faint images' of these impressions. Consequently, there cannot be 'abstract ideas' in the sense in which this term is used by Locke. There can be only general *terms*. We can have an 'impression' of a triangle and an idea of a triangle, but we cannot have an idea of the triangle *in specie*. The representative of generality is the general term, in our case the word 'triangle', which we have learned to associate with the objects belonging to the class of triangles. Hume[2] points out that 'we do not annex distinct and complete ideas to every term we make use of'. We use many general terms in our daily conversation without associating with them any distinct ideas and yet we are quite able to use them correctly and in the right context. A general term, according to Hume is not a linguistic sign pointing to an 'abstract idea' or some other abstruse entity, but a word which in the ordinary business of life we have grown accustomed to associate with certain objects, events, actions, etc.

Similarity is the key concept in the theory of abstraction by which Hume tries to explain the genesis of general terms. According to him, it is our ability to isolate the similarities among things that makes classification possible and explains the generality of general terms. We shall return to this problem later on. What is important is that Hume utterly rejects 'abstract ideas' or any similar 'abstract entities'. He emphasises the role of words as instruments of generality and points out that the contexts in which certain words are habitually used help to convey what these words mean.

All this shows that there is no place for Husserl's 'general objects' in Hume's universe. Hume would reject Husserl's 'general objects' just as he rejected Locke's 'abstract ideas'. This is equally true of Berkeley. At the same time, it cannot be denied that both Hume's and Berkeley's arguments contain many weak points, and Husserl, as we shall see presently, found little difficulty in showing that the explanation they gave of general terms leaves much to be desired. Husserl accepts the essentials of their criticism of Locke's theory of

[1] Berkeley, *A Treatise concerning the Principles of Human Knowledge*, Introduction, sect. XII.
[2] See *A Treatise of Human Nature,* bk. I, pt. I, sect. VII.

'abstract ideas', but he emphatically denies that a nominalistic solution of the kind they propose represents a satisfactory answer to the problem. It is not enough to say, he maintains, that an idea can serve as a representative of a certain class of ideas, or to appeal to similarities, or to say that a general term is in a great many cases understood from the contexts in which it is customarily used. None of this can explain how the meaning of a general term can preserve its identity or how two individual objects, say, two different patches of colour, can exemplify the *same* universal—namely the colour that they have in common. The ideal identity of meanings and species remain a mystery to empiricism.

Criticism of Berkeley's idea of representation

The fallacy of nominalism, according to Husserl, is that it tries to explain 'general objects' in terms of individual objects and their relations, overlooking or ignoring the categorial difference between these two types of objects. The controversy over 'abstract ideas' illustrates the kind of confusion arising from this fallacy. The meaning of a general term is not something that is extracted by a process of abstraction from a class of physically similar objects. It is certainly not a kind of image in our mind that loosely fits a number of similar individuals. Berkeley was right to attack Locke's 'abstract ideas', but his own theory of representation, in Husserl's view, shows an equal misunderstanding of the problem. Berkeley thought that in order to achieve generality it is sufficient to regard an idea as a representative of the class of ideas that are all 'of the same sort'. But, says Husserl, the word 'representative' here is misleading. This word is used in the sense of someone representing someone else, someone performing a function which otherwise someone else would have to perform. But who is here this 'someone else'? On Berkeley's view, any idea from a certain class of ideas can with equal justification serve as a representative of that class. They all, in principle, have equal status, which means that they all can be regarded as 'representatives' and as individuals in their own right. But the question is *what* do they represent? Since the class is not itself an object, it is difficult to see what they can in fact represent except themselves, and so we are back where we started. Clearly, the idea of representation cannot help us to explain the phenomenon of generality; on the contrary, we must be able to understand generality in order to be able to understand the meaning of representation.

The meaning of a general term cannot depend on any particular idea that we may or may not have in our mind. The meaning of the word 'triangle', Husserl points out, remains the same no matter

whether this word conjures up in our mind an image of an equilateral, scalene, isosceles or some other triangle. In fact, as Hume
rightly observed, we do not have to have any particular image in
our mind in order to be able to use a given word correctly. This
alone shows that meaning cannot lie in the representation of some
ideas by others. Meaning, Husserl maintains, has nothing to do
with ideas or images. This does not mean that we would be able to
understand what the word 'triangle' means without ever having
seen a triangle. Of course we must have some experience of triangles
or triangular objects. But triangles that we may see or imagine must
not be confused with the *meaning* of the word 'triangle'. A concrete
triangle is a mere illustration of the meaning of the general term.
It is just an 'example'. These examples may be indispensable for
our apprehending the universals which they exemplify, but it is
none the less important to make a clear distinction between the two.

But, it might be asked, is this distinction a good enough reason
for adopting the view that the meanings of general terms are what
Husserl calls 'ideal-identical unities' whose identity remains unaffec-
ted by the circumstances in which these terms are used? Berkeley
points out that meanings of such terms may fluctuate considerably.
We tend to think that every such term has or ought to have a
definite and settled meaning, but in fact their meanings often vary
in different contexts. In Berkeley's view, 'there is no such thing as
one precise and definite signification annexed to any general name'.[1]
But if this is so, all talk of ideal-identical meanings and ideal-
identical species would seem to make little sense.

Husserl agrees that words may alter their meanings. A 'general
name' can change its meaning, there can be no doubt about this.
Sometimes we make such a change ourselves by arbitrary convention.
But, Husserl points out, we must not forget that it is *words* that we
are here talking about. Meanings themselves do not change, it is
words that change their meanings; and it is because meanings remain
identical that we can detect and define such a change.

Objections to Hume's theory of abstraction
We turn now to Husserl's criticism of Hume.

According to Hume, the 'ideas' that we have differ in their
vividness but they are always concrete. It is only through reflection
upon these ideas that we can form some kind of abstract notions,
by distinguishing and classifying the various resemblances between
these ideas. Hume explains this in the following way. Suppose we
have two globes of marble, one black and one white, and a cube of
white marble. It is obvious that we can classify these three objects

[1] *Principles of Human Knowledge*, Introduction, sect. XVIII.

in different ways, according to their different resemblances. If we take shape as a principle of selection the two globes will go together; if, on the other hand, we base our selection on colour, the white globe and the white cube will form a group despite the difference in their shapes. The classification clearly will depend on the *aspect* under which we consider the given objects. The objects themselves remain the same as before. A globe of black marble remains a globe and black no matter which class it is in. It is only the aspect under which we look at it that changes.

Husserl does not accept this analysis. In his view, all this is totally inadequate to explain general terms. Hume based his explanation on the relation of similarity without realising the importance of the objectifying intentional acts. There is something more fundamental than the relation of similarity, namely the intentional distinction between appearance and what *appears* in appearance. In Husserl's view, one of Hume's biggest mistakes was that he allowed these two things to merge into one. He failed to distinguish between a perception and what is apperceived in the perception, between an 'idea' and the intentional object that we have in this idea. To take Hume's own example, it is according to Husserl necessary to distinguish between the 'globe-appearance' and the 'appearing *globe*', the latter being the intentional object. The distinction, claims Husserl, would be necessary even if the globe were imaginary. The intentional object is not to be confused with the physical object. The question whether a given object really exists or not is a separate question which does not affect this distinction.

Now just as we can perceive an individual object we can, according to Husserl, also 'perceive', though in acts of a different kind, a 'general object' in a single empirical datum. Thus within a perceptual whole, say, that of a globe-*appearance*, various 'parts' can be distinguished from each other (such as colour, shape, etc.). In a special act in which we direct ourselves upon one constituent part of this experiential whole (e.g. the white of the globe-*appearance*) we can, according to Husserl, 'apperceive' the relevant attribute as an object. In short, Husserl maintains against Hume that we can get hold of a 'general object' *directly* through a special act directed upon the perception of one single empirical object and that the relation of similarity will help us little without such an act.

One of the most deep-seated empiricist prejudices, from Husserl's point of view, is that meanings of general terms can be explained in terms of the latter's extensions. In trying to explain the meaning of a term one tends to look for objects of which this term can be predicated. But what happens if one does not find any objects? What about the meaning of empty terms? Faced with this difficulty one

tends to seek refuge in propositions. Terms, it is said, mean something only in the context of true or false propositions. But this, of
course, does not remove the difficulty about meaning, for such
terms can also occur in propositions which are meaningful but not
necessarily true or false. How, then, are we to explain meaning?
How do we decide when a term or a propositions is meaningful?
Husserl's own answer to this question is that all expressions are
meaningful provided they do not violate the basic laws of what he
calls the 'logical grammar' and can be apprehended as 'semantic
unities'. Whether a given expression is applicable to anything is a
separate question. According to Husserl, the absence of 'fulfilment'
in a given case does not render the relevant expression meaningless.
This, he argues, does not happen even in the cases where a fulfilment
is logically impossible. Expressions such as 'round square', 'The
first prime is green' or 'My hat is virtuous' cannot be simply dismissed as meaningless, for it is only because we *understand* what
they *mean* that we know that they cannot be true of anything. They
are all *syntactically* well-formed and intelligible expressions, although
the meaning-intentions which they express are incapable of fulfilment.
According to Husserl, it is important to distinguish these and
similar expressions from nonsensical phrases such as 'This hat no
is and' which as wholes are incapable of meaning, and therefore
cannot be regarded as expressions at all.

As far as the meanings of terms such as *red, white, globe, triangle,*
etc., are concerned, Husserl's view is that no empiricist theory of
abstraction will help us to understand them unless we have understood the difference between the ideally posited universal and its
spatio-temporal 'examples'. This, according to Husserl, we can do
only through an 'ideating abstraction' or 'ideation'. In an 'act of
ideation' that we perform on an object, or rather on an experience
in which we have something as an object, the existential aspect
recedes into the background, and it is because the existential aspect
recedes into the background that, according to Husserl, we are able
to penetrate down to the 'essence'. 'Species', according to Husserl,
are discovered in just such 'acts of ideation'. 'Thus'—he writes—'we
apprehend the species *red* directly, in itself as it were, on the basis
of a single perception of something red. We look at the red colour
of an object as given to us in a perception, but we do this in a special
kind of act; an act which aims at the 'ideal', the 'universal'. The
abstraction in the sense of this act is completely different from mere
pointing out or separating the perceived red from the rest of the
perceptual context. In order to point out this difference we have
repeatedly spoken of the *ideating* or generalising abstraction.'[1]

[1] *Logische Untersuchungen,* vol. II/1, p. 223.

One thing that seems fairly certain is that it is not enough to appeal to similarity when trying to explain the meaning of a general term. If by saying that this globe of marble is white I only mean to say that its colour resembles the colour of other white things, I shall, as Husserl observed, find myself involved in an infinite regress. All I shall be able to say will be that something is white because something else is white, and so on *ad infinitum*. But it is clear that a recourse to similarly coloured things so far from explaining the predicate 'white' presupposes in fact that we know how to use it. We must be able to make a distinction between the whiteness and the sensations of white. The mere comparison of white things with one another will not result in an understanding of the concept unless we have made a distinction between the sensations and the intentionally apperceived *white*.

Husserl concludes from this that all attempts to explain meanings of general terms in terms of sets of similar sensations or similar 'ideas' must be rejected as inadequate and misleading. The basis of our understanding of generality and identity of meaning, according to him, are acts that can be performed already at the level of very simple experiences. 'General objects' become accessible to us through such acts. The empiricist theories of abstraction, according to Husserl, fail to give a satisfactory explanation of meaning because they ignore such acts and because they are unable to understand the role of 'ideating abstraction' or 'ideation'. It should be made clear that this act of 'ideation', to Husserl, is not a kind of 'sixth sense'. He regards it as an act of reason by which, as it were, we extract an essence from a concrete experience and posit it *qua* essence; an act by which we 'turn things into examples'.

6

PHENOMENOLOGICAL REDUCTION AND

HUSSERL'S IDEA OF A

TRANSCENDENTAL PHILOSOPHY

Our discussion so far has revealed three important features of Husserl's phenomenological approach. First, he regards intentional experiences as the basic material of philosophical analysis. The phenomenon of intentionality is to him of central importance and he thinks that this phenomenon should be studied carefully if we are to be able to clarify not only the philosophical foundations of logic but also the noetic conditions of knowledge in general. Secondly, he insists on the fundamental distinction between empirical individuals and what he calls 'general objects'. He subsequently[1] rephrased this distinction in a more general form as a distinction between 'facts' and 'essences' (the latter including all kinds of species, sortal and adjectival universals and their genera, propositional meanings, etc.). Thirdly, he thinks that an epistemological analysis of logic and its foundations must be kept free from empirical existential considerations if it is to avoid relativism and psychologism and produce solid results.

The point mentioned last gives some, though not a complete, idea of what is involved in the so-called 'phenomenological reduction'—a method which Husserl first presented in a series of lectures in 1907 and made extensive use of in his *Ideas for a Pure Phenomenology and Phenomenological Philosophy* (1913). The method was intended to clear the last obstacles standing in the way of an adequate

---

[1] See *Ideen zu einer reinen Phänomenologie und phänomenologischen Philosophie.* Part One of *Ideen* was first published in 1913. Part Two and Part Three were published posthumously together with a new edition of Part One in *Husserliana*, vols. III, IV and V (Haag, Martinus Nijhoff, 1950). I shall quote from this edition.

philosophical understanding of the noetic conditions of knowledge and to lay firm foundations for a comprehensive *transcendental phenomenological philosophy*. We must now say something about this method.

Generally speaking the method of phenomenological reduction is a means of detecting what is constitutive and essential in our cognitive relationship with the world. It is a way of discovering the basic 'phenomenological facts' that make knowledge and the world as we know it possible. There are different degrees of reduction and Husserl often speaks of 'phenomenological reductions' in the plural, although with regard to what he calls their 'unity as a whole' he normally uses the singular form preceded by a definite article.

One form of reduction with which we are already familiar is a reduction or a 'suspension' of the empirical in the case of logical objects. We saw that in an act of *ideation* the empirical existential aspect fades into the background to reveal the non-spatio-temporal 'general object', the 'essence'. I can claim that I have understood the meaning of $2+3=5$ only when I have understood that this truth is not dependent on the existence of these signs, or on its being expressed in this particular way, or on my own existence and my ability to understand what the above expression means.

However, according to Husserl, a much more radical type of reduction is required if we are to be able to explain the ultimate presuppositions of knowledge. The reduction that he has in mind involves a suspension of *all* empirical existential considerations and of *all a priori* assumptions about entities external (transcendent) to experiences. The idea behind Husserl's phenomenological reduction is that we should concentrate on what is immanently given in our own 'stream of experiences', treating these experiences not as empirical events in a 'natural world' but as *intentional structures* to be clarified in a 'phenomenological reflection'. (We shall return to this later.) Husserl wants us to go back to what is essential, basic, irreducible in our experiences. The 'phenomenological reduction' is designed to help us in this. Its effect, according to Husserl, is to transform the consciousness in the sense of a 'stream of experiences', my own consciousness, into a *transcendental* consciousness, i.e. into a stream of 'transcendentally purified' (or transcendentially reduced') experiences. This 'transcendental consciousness', he maintains, remains as a 'phenomenological residuum' after the reduction, and, according to him, it is here, in the region of our 'transcendental consciousness' or 'transcendental subjectivity', that a genuine *phenomenological constitution* (phenomenologico-philosophical 'reconstruction') of the world must begin.

Husserl's method of radical reduction is reminiscent in many ways

C

of the Cartesian method of doubt. But before comparing Husserl's and Descartes' methods and their respective philosophical positions we must say a few more words about the reduction generally. What is important to bear in mind is that for Husserl the reduction is not only a means of detecting the essential structures of intentional phenomena but also an instrument for combatting psychologism. The reduction, according to Husserl, enables one to dispense with all genetic and existential considerations and to concentrate on the analysis of the 'eidetic structures' of experiences. Thus interpreted the reduction clearly becomes something very different from what is known under the same name in Logical Positivism. It might perhaps be useful at this point to try and explain briefly the differences between these two types of reduction, for this will at the same time illustrate the gulf that divides *phenomenology* from *phenomenalism*.

The positivist and the phenomenological reduction

The phenomenalism of the positivists goes back to Mach and Berkeley. It emerged partly from the criticism of the doctrine of substance and has remained essentially an anti-substance doctrine. In Berkeley's philosophy this criticism, admittedly, was directed only against the idea of a material substance, but from his premises there seemed to be only a short step to the rejection of substance altogether. If, as Berkeley maintained, the meaning of existence is to be explained in terms of the (real or ideal) possibility of perception, the assumption of the existence of an unperceivable substratum makes no sense. It is only things that we can meaningfully speak of as existent—it was said—and things are nothing but 'complexes of sensations'.

In positivist philosophy the acceptance of phenomenalism was closely linked with the principle of *verification*. The principle requires that all meaningful empirical statements should be verifiable and since the verification of such statements depends ultimately on the occurrence of certain sense-data it somehow seemed natural to think that things, in so far as they can be experienced, are in fact composed of sense-data. In the linguistic version of phenomenalism this belief was expressed in the assertion that all statements about physical objects can be translated into statements about sense-data or 'sense-contents'. According to the so-called 'equivalence theory' every empirical statement about things is equivalent to a set of statements about sense-contents. The statement 'I am now writing with a ball-point pen', according to this theory, is in principle translatable into a set of statements in which all words refer to sense-contents and no ball-point pen is mentioned.

This Husserl most decisively rejects. Although himself an opponent of the metaphysical doctrine of substance he regards the phenomenalist reduction as an unsuitable and mistaken approach to the problem. As we can already guess, his main objection to phenomenalism is that the latter tries to explain meaning in terms of sense-contents instead of in terms of meaning-giving and meaning-fulfilling acts. Phenomenalism, according to Husserl, is unable to discover or understand the 'essentially given' in experiences because it misinterprets the meaning of experience. Its reduction, as it were, points in the wrong direction.

We saw that Husserl made a distinction between signs as marks and signs as expressions. Expressions are meaning-carrying signs; marks, on the other hand, have a function comparable to that of tags that are sometimes attached to objects for the purpose of easy identification. Phenomenalists, Husserl would say, tend to mistake words for such tags. They forget that in language we operate with expressions and that these expressions carry meanings in virtue of certain signifying acts. The signifying intention often changes and with it the expression changes too, although the sense-content need not change. Between a sense-content and an expression there is always interpolated a meaning-giving act. After all, I need not call this thing in my hand a 'ball-point pen'. I may call it a 'biro' or invent for it some other ugly name.

This indicates the complex structure of the experience in which we relate ourselves to an object. In the example just given we have to distinguish, for every description used, between an intentional act and its objective meaning-content as conveyed in that particular description, quite apart from the sensory content of experience which may or may not change. These distinctions remain in force whether the object aimed at actually exists or not.

For suppose I am dreaming and the pen in my hand is not real at all. I shall still be able to make the same distinctions. Or suppose I am merely wishing to hold a pen in my hand. Here too I shall be able to distinguish between the act and its objective 'meaning-content'. Husserl used the terms 'noesis' and 'noema' to designate these two aspects of an intentional experience. To different noetic acts or 'noeses' there corresponds, according to him, different 'noematic correlates'. 'Noesis' and 'noema' must of course be strictly distinguished from the sensory content of an experience.

Husserl kept changing and modifying his terminology as he went on perfecting and expanding his phenomenological analysis and it might be useful at this point to mention the more important terms he introduced in his mature 'transcendental' period. Some of these terms have a conspicuously Aristotelian ring about them. Thus he calls the purely sensorial non-intentional component of an experience *hyle*. This 'amorphous' sensory stuff, according to him, is shaped by the intentional *morphé*. Here we have a new version of the old distinction between *matter* and *form*. The amorphous *hyle* is brought to life, as it were, by the intentional form-giving acts. The intentional and strictly non-material component of an experience is described by Husserl as *noesis*. This word is related to *nous* (reason) and this relationship acquires now a deeper philosophical significance. Husserl looks at *noeses* as 'specifications of *nous*'. Finally, there is the *noema* as the ideal (*ideell*) content-correlate of *noesis*, often referred to as the 'noematic content' or 'noematic meaning'. Even a simple perception, according to Husserl, has its *noema*: it is *the perceived as such*. (In our earlier example 'this ball-point pen' and 'this biro' express the noematic meanings of relevant perceptions). In an act of recollection the noema is *the remembered as such*. In expectation the noema is *the expected as such*. In judging it is *the judged as such*, etc. This 'as such' points already to a reduction to 'essences'.

Here once again the difference between the phenomenological and the phenomenalist approach becomes apparent. The phenomenalist's aim is to find a method of reducing all statements about objects to statements about sense-contents. The phenomenologist, on the other hand, tries to analyse the various types of intentional experiences and to describe their intentional *structure*. In order to be able to accomplish this task successfully, he must, according to Husserl, perform the 'phenomenological reduction', that is, set aside all existential considerations concerning the objects of his experience. He must suspend all judgements about spatio-temporal existence of such objects. Consequently, the reduction does not mean here a reduction to statements about sense-contents, or empirical things, but a reduction to what constitutes the essential features of intentional experiences.

The phenomenologist is interested in describing the essential structures of concrete 'situations'. These structures, according to Husserl, can be discovered only after the existential aspect of these 'situations' has been temporarily neutralised. What we must do, according to him, is to focus our attention (in phenomenological reflection) on the aspect of meaning. In this way only, he maintains, we shall be able to isolate and describe the basic 'phenomenological facts'.

Whereas the phenomenalist's phenomena are sense-contents, the phenomenologist's 'phenomena' are what Husserl calls the 'noetic-noematic structures' of intentional experiences. This indicates the depth of the gulf that divides their respective positions. From the phenomenologist's standpoint, the phenomenalist is engaged in a hopeless task of trying to explain the meaning of what we say about the world around us in terms of the existence of certain sense-contents, acting very much like someone who is trying to explain a picture in terms of the *material* of which the picture is made instead of concentrating on what the picture *means*.

The process of reduction

The process of reduction to the phenomenologically essential can begin already at the level of the most ordinary experiences. Take, for example, a simple perceptual experience such as my seeing this chair in front of me. I assume that there is something 'out there', an object called 'chair' which I can see and touch and which I can use for certain purposes. But suppose I now disregard the transcendent object chair and concentrate on what is immediately given in my experience of seeing a chair. I find myself now at a different level and my attitude changes. I am no longer looking at the chair as an object 'out there' on which I can put my books or on which I can climb to screw a bulb into the lamp holder. I become aware of my having something as an object which I recognise *as a chair*. I do not merely have a chair-percept; my experience does not consist merely of certain sensations. I become aware of what the percept means. I can distinguish in my experience between a sense-content and a 'noematic content'. And this distinction remains preserved no matter whether the perceived chair is real or imaginary.

I am now free to posit the 'noematic content' of what I see as an ideal object, ideal essence, because by drawing this distinction I am, as it were, stepping out of the immediate existential context and entering a new relationship with the world around me. By the same token I am now free—according to Husserl—to posit an Ego as an idealised projection of my own self. By doing all this I am not denying or ignoring the existence of anything. I am only suspending existential considerations about objects transcending experiences for the time being, and this is precisely what phenomenological reduction is about.

All this gives a clear indication of the general drift of Husserl's argument. It also reveals the first contours of the problem to which he is led by his argument. It is clear, for example, that his insistence on the suspension of existential empirical considerations as a first step towards discovering the essential structures of intentional experiences and making clear the presuppositions of knowledge in general commits him not only to a rejection of phenomenalism, but also to a rejection of all theories which make the assumption of the existence of a physical reality independent of ourselves the basis of an explanation of meaning and truth. From Husserl's standpoint, an object is constituted as an object in an *intentional act*; consequently we can talk of a 'reality of objects' only as a correlate of an intentional consciousness. This puts a new complexion on the problem of truth. Truth, it seems, can now be defined in terms of what is evident to this consciousness. But the crucial question is what status does this consciousness have. If it is an empirical, 'psychological' consciousness, it will be impossible to assert the universality and objective validity of any truth; for what is evident to me need not be evident to anyone else. This is one more reason why Husserl finds it necessary to introduce the concept of a 'transcendental consciousness'.

In *Logical Investigations* he attacked psychologism and very much like Frege defended the objectivity and apodicticity of logical truth. Now he takes a critical attitude very reminiscent of Kant and tries to combine the 'objectivity of truth' with the idea of 'transcendental subjectivity'. One could perhaps describe Husserl's new position by saying that he tried to unite Frege's logical objectivism with Brentano's intentionality on a Kantian basis.

But we must now consider Husserl's radical reduction and its implications.

The transcendental epoché

When Husserl thinks of the reduction in the transcendental sense he usually uses the Greek word *epoché*. The phenomenological *epoché* means the suspension of *all* judgements concerning the spatio-temporal existence of things which I assume to be 'out there'; it involves a suspension, or perhaps we should say a radical modification, of what Husserl calls the 'natural standpoint'. We have partly explained what this means when discussing the example of a chair. The difference now is only that the change of attitude affects the *whole* spatio-temporal fact-world which I find 'continually present and facing me', the world to which 'I myself belong, as do all other men' and which I find to be 'out there'.[1] In other words, the change is now more radical.

The essence of the so-called 'natural standpoint' is that it takes the presence of this world for granted. The only problems that we encounter from the 'natural standpoint', according to Husserl, are those of finding adequate methods for establishing causal relationships within this world, and for organising facts in its various regions. This is of course precisely what the natural sciences (i.e. the 'sciences of the natural standpoint') are trying to do. But while the natural scientist automatically assumes the existence of an

[1] See *Ideen*, I, p. 63.

objective fact-world 'out there' the philosopher asks how is such a world possible. The task of philosophy, maintains Husserl, is to try to explain what is basically involved in our relationship with the world, how the world comes into being, as it were, and this requires that we should radically alter our attitude. We must 'disconnect' the thesis of the 'natural standpoint', or, in Husserl's favourite expression, we must put it in 'brackets'. We do not have to deny the existence of the fact-world; in fact, we do not have to deny anything at all. All we have to do is to refrain from making any judgements concerning the 'things out there' in their spatio-temporal existence. This is the gist of his *epoché*.

Husserl's general aim is to clarify what is involved in our relationship with an objective world through an analysis of the 'noetic-noematic' structures of experiences. He thinks that these structures are obscured from our view in the 'world of the natural standpoint' and he maintains that they must be brought out of this obscurity and elucidated if we are to understand how we know what we know, and how the knowledge of a world is possible at all. Phenomenological reduction, according to him, is the key to this understanding. It makes it possible for us to describe the 'pure facts' at a meta-empirical level. As a universal *epoché* the phenomenological reduction, according to Husserl, takes us back philosophically to the 'absolute beginning'. It takes us into the region of 'transcendental consciousness', the region, that is, of 'transcendentally purified' experiences, and the transcendental *Ego* as a unity of these experiences; or, in more simple language, it makes the one who performs the reduction, myself, realise the fundamental meaning of the fact that I *have conscious experiences*, that I *think;* and, according to Husserl, once I have been made aware by the *epoché* of the fundamental meaning and the irreducibility of this fact I am ready to begin the process of 'phenomenological constitution' of the world in transcendental terms.

All this of course points back to Descartes. Descartes made a similar philosophical experiment and Husserl himself draws attention to this similarity. But he also points out important differences between his and Descartes' position. Descartes' main concern was to establish what we can truly say we know for certain. And he used *doubt* as a methodical device in trying to discover this certainty. If we try to doubt everything, including the existence of a world 'out there', we shall as a result discover our doubting (and therefore thinking) ego as something whose existence cannot be doubted, something that indubitably exists and cannot be 'eliminated' with the rest. Husserl's *epoché* does not have exactly the same function. In the act in which the thesis of the 'natural standpoint' is 'disconnected' nothing is denied, the existence of the world is not doubted, only the judgements about it are suspended. *Epoché* does not provisionally 'eliminate' the world of things as the Cartesian doubt does; it only changes our viewpoint and makes it possible to regard our experiences in a different light. The Cartesian doubt, according to Husserl, is 'one attempt at universal denial'; the *epoché* on the other hand, implies merely the setting aside of the thesis of the 'natural standpoint', rendering this thesis inoperative, so that we may concentrate on the analysis of what is essentially involved in intentional experiences and explain what Husserl calls the 'meaning' of the world by clarifying this world's 'transcendental origins'.

But the consequences of an act of *epoché* are more far-reaching than might at first appear. For one thing, by rendering the thesis of the 'natural standpoint' inoperative by putting this thesis 'out of action', such an act at once removes the natural sciences from the philosophical horizon. This may look an alarming prospect. To Husserl, it is something that has to be accepted as part of the programme of reduction. 'Thus'—he writes—'I *disconnect all sciences relating to this natural world,* much as I trust them, much as I admire them and have not the least intention of objecting to them in any way. I make *absolutely no use of their standards. I do not adopt a single one of their propositions however evident these propositions may be; I take none of them, no one of these propositions serves me as a foundation*—that is, as long as such a proposition is understood in the way in which it is understood in the relevant scientific context, namely as a truth about certain *concrete facts* in this world.'[1] He does not doubt the value of natural sciences, but he thinks that these sciences, being the sciences of the 'natural standpoint', cannot help us to understand the world *philosophically.* They cannot do so as long as they make implicit and unexplained assumptions about the existence of an 'external' world. The task of the *epoché* is to 'remedy' this situation and to open up what he calls a 'new region of being' which is not empirical but transcendental.

But the suspension of the existential assumptions about the 'natural world' is only the first in a *series* of 'transcendental reductions'. According to Husserl, the radical reduction, the radical *epoché*, affects not only the natural sciences; it affects also what he calls the 'eidetic sciences' such as logic and pure mathematics: we are not allowed to make use of their deductive methods in our transcendental analysis. All this goes into the brackets together with our own empirical ego. What remains are the 'transcendentally purified' experiences and the 'transcendental Ego', and in exploring this region we can, it seems, rely only on self-evidence and on what

[1] ibid., p. 68.

Husserl calls 'intuition of essences' (*Wesenserchauung*); but since these concepts too must be transcendentally interpreted, i.e. purified from any psychological or historical references, it is difficult to see how I can ever hope to know that in my analysis I am not in fact following the wrong path.

Husserl's method of reduction clearly poses a number of serious problems. The transition from the empirical to the transcendental level effected by the *epoché* is far from clear and Husserl has left a host of questions unanswered. For example, how can the action of the one who actually performs the reduction be explained in transcendental terms? I am asked to set aside all existential empirical considerations, all existential assumptions about historical entities or events; but this itself is a historical decision taken by a historical being and it is difficult to see how this can be explained on a transcendental basis. It seems that we cannot after all put in brackets all existential considerations about the historical world. But if this is so, there seems to be little justification for insisting on the necessity of a radically 'transcendental approach'.

The transcendental phenomenological reduction is supposed to help reveal the essential and irreducible presuppositions of knowledge by providing an access to the essential structures of experiences and the basic patterns of interrelationships obtaining between these experiences. This, according to Husserl, is possible only if all empirical existential assumptions are put in 'brackets'. Once this is done, Husserl claims, intentional experiences become describable in their 'eidetic purity'. But what exactly does it mean to say that intentional experiences become describable in their 'eidetic purity'? A radical application of the reduction has the effect of transforming these experiences into certain noetic-noematic structures in which both the acts and the noematic contents are completely de-materialised. But how exactly are these de-materialised structures of concrete experiences to be described and, above all, how is their link with the actual world to be clarified and maintained?

Husserl's biggest problem arising from the *epoché* is how to re-discover the real (historical) world once this world has been put in 'brackets', that is, once its existence is no longer accepted as a primitive fact but regarded rather as a 'possibility' to be explained in transcendental terms.

7

REASON AND REALITY

The doctrine of transcendental phenomenological reduction marked a new stage in Husserl's philosophical development. It involved a considerable modification of the position from which he wrote his *Logical Investigations* and represented a crucial step in his own philosophical transformation from a descriptive psychologist into a transcendental philosopher. Husserl did not abandon the phenomenological approach. He did not abandon intentionality. He only felt that as a result of the reduction he was able to conduct his phenomenological analysis at a more fundamental level.

Husserl's labyrinthine prose and the complexity of his analysis sometimes make it difficult to follow his argument and his *Ideas* in particular does not make easy reading. But the general direction in which he is moving is clear enough. We saw earlier that his overriding interest was in explaining the relation between the subjective and the objective aspect of knowledge, or, more generally, between the subjective and the objective aspect of meaning. This, he now thought could be done successfully only on a transcendental basis, by showing how the world itself could be constituted as a *transcendental system*. The result was his 'transcendental-phenomenological idealism'—an ambitiously conceived programme of 'phenomenological constitution' of the various aspects of reality which plunged Husserl into difficulties and problems with which he struggled unsuccessfully for the rest of his life.

The effect of the transcendental reduction, inevitably, was to give his analysis a new meaning. In the *Logical Investigations* Husserl's approach was phenomenological but not transcendental (in the sense explained in the preceding chapter) and he expressly criticised the idea of a 'pure Ego'. At that time phenomenology was still conceived by him as a 'method' rather than as a 'theory'. Now he regards phenomenology as a theoretical discipline in its own right —as the *fundamental* philosophical discipline, to be precise. His phenomenology now combines the roles of a critique of knowledge and a transcendental ontology.

In *Logical Investigations* Husserl had more modest aims. He was trying to clarify the epistemological presuppositions of logic through a phenomenological analysis of the 'phenomenon of meaning'. Now he is trying to clarify the transcendental presuppositions of knowledge in general and at the same time to show how the structure of the 'objective world' can be explained ('constituted') in transcendental terms from a transcendental basis. He is embarking, in fact, on an idealist programme of exhibiting the 'reason in the reality'. But, as we shall see, there were more difficulties than he anticipated.

The ambiguity of Husserl's idealism

Let us take a closer look at the nature of his 'transcendental' approach.

The basic principle by which Husserl is guided and which he regards as an essential feature of the 'scientific method' is this. If we want to understand a phenomenon we must inquire into its origin and ask what are the conditions that make such a phenomenon possible. Scientifically speaking we can claim to have understood a phenomenon when we have understood it as a *possibility* in accordance with a certain law. Husserl tries to make a similar point in the context of his transcendental analysis. What he wants to say, in very general terms, is that we can understand the phenomenon *world* when we are in the position to explain it as a possibility in accordance with certain *transcendental* laws. What we must do is to try to explain its 'origin' and its structure in *transcendental terms*. This inevitably reminds one of Kant.

In the period between 1901 and 1907 Husserl studied Kant with great care and was influenced by him profoundly. But although Kant's 'transcendental approach' appealed to him, he thought that Kant in his analysis did not go as far as he might have done. Kant, in his view, was not 'radical enough'. Kant, says Husserl, discovered the region of 'transcendental subjectivity', but he failed to exploit this discovery in the right way. Both in his general attitude and in his method of reasoning he was still too much dependent on the old rationalist metaphysics to be able to understand the phenomeno-logical structure of this subjectivity and to appreciate fully the implications of the intimate connection between the structure of subjectivity and the structure of the 'world'. Kant's inability to rid himself completely of metaphysical prejudices was demonstrated by his doctrine of the 'Thing in itself'. According to Kant, the world as it is in itself is inaccessible to, and exists independently of, the cognitive subject. This meant that there was a permanent and unbridgeable gulf between what can be known and what exists in itself. The 'transcendental subjectivity' was thus separated from the noumenal world and a permanent cleavage was created between 'reason' and 'reality'. This, maintained Husserl, was where Kant erred. Kant's critique was not 'phenomenological' enough. From Husserl's standpoint, a transcendental critique of knowledge is part of a phenomenological 'theory of the world' and can fulfil its task adequately only within the context of a transcendental phenomenological *ontology*.

But while critical of what he regarded as a lack of phenomenological consistency in Kant's transcendental approach, Husserl is much more critical of those anti-Kantians who dispute the value or question the possibility of an *a priori* transcendental analysis. Once again he turns against the empiricists as the chief offenders. Empiricism, to him, is inextricably intertwined with relativism and scepticism and he has no patience for either. One of the main reasons why the empiricists are unable to understand the transcendental standpoint, maintains Husserl, is their fundamental misconception about the structure of basic 'data'. His view (as made clear in the preceding chapters) is that the empiricists, as a rule, give a wrong analysis of experience. They do not understand either the role or the importance of acts and the 'intuition of essences'. As a result, they are unable to give an adequate account of the conditions that make experience and knowledge possible. Their approach being non-phenomenological, they fail to understand either the purpose or the importance of the phenomenological reduction.

Husserl himself regards the phenomenological reduction in the sense of transcendental *epoché* as a passport to genuine philosophy. In the act of *epoché*, he maintains, we rid ourselves at one blow of all metaphysical and empiricist misconceptions. We discover the region of transcendental consciousness from where the world can be described in all its essential aspects adequately and without bias. We realise that the world has a transcendental structure and that it can be made fully intelligible only from the standpoint of the 'transcendental subjectivity'. This is the gist of his mature philosophical position to which he refers as 'transcendental-phenomenological idealism'.

But this name conceals an ambiguity. For Husserl's 'transcendental idealism', as has been made clear, is concerned not only with

knowledge but with the 'structure of the world'. The word 'transcendental' was used by Kant in relation to knowledge; but Husserl
gives it an ontological significance. In fact, although he describes
his mature philosophy as 'transcendental-phenomenological' it is
clear that this philosophy has the makings of an idealist metaphysics.
The effect of his radical reduction was to institute the 'transcendental
consciousness', the 'transcendental subjectivity', as a phenomenological and metaphysical Ultimate, as something which unlike the
spatio-temporal world cannot be put in 'brackets' or removed in
any way, as something, in fact, on which everything else depends for
existence.

The transcendental reduction and 'external world'

But the problem was how to reconstruct the spatio-temporal world
on this basis. According to Husserl, the *epoché* yields us a purified
concept of consciousness and '. . . consciousness considered in its
"purity" must be accepted as a *self-contained realm of being,* as a
realm of *absolute being,* into which nothing can penetrate and from
which nothing can escape, a realm which has no 'external' spatio-
temporal dimension and cannot be part of any spatio-temporal context, which cannot causally influence, or be causally influenced by,
anything—provided that causality is taken in the normal sense of
natural causality, that is, as a relation of dependence between items
of the actual world.'[1]

As a result of *epoché*, then, consciousness—in the sense of a
'stream of experiences'—becomes a 'self-contained realm of being',
a realm of 'absolute being'. 'Absolute'—because *epoché*, according
to Husserl, shows that conscious experiences are not necessarily
dependent for their existence on anything *external* to themselves.
The view that Husserl is trying to put forward, in effect, is that there
is no relation of logical dependence between my having conscious
experiences and there being things in physical space and time. To
him, '. . . the whole *spatio-temporal world* in which man and the
human Ego view themselves as subordinate realities is *such that
it has merely intentional existence*; in other words, it exists in a
secondary, relative sense of the word, i.e. *for* a consciousness. . . . It
is such that consciousness posits its existence in experience and is,
in principle, intuitable and determinable only as the identical reference point of the harmoniously motivated experiential manifolds,
but beyond this it is nothing at all; more accurately, it would be an
absurdity to suppose that it could be anything else beyond this.'[2]

But if this is so, can we be sure that there is an 'external' spatio-

---

[1] *Ideen,* I, p. 117.
[2] ibid.

temporal world at all? What sense is there in supposing that there is such a world? Husserl insists that by suspending the realist thesis of the 'natural standpoint' we are not *denying* or even *doubting* the existence of an external world. But while this may be so, while the radical reduction may not actually involve an act of denial or doubt, its effect is certainly to make it impossible to show that such a world could exist except as an 'intentional object of consciousness'. But, one might ask, if only intentional, why real rather than fictional?

Husserl finds himself here in a serious difficulty. He insists that the world of spatio-temporal things exists merely in a dependent sense and that only consciousness (taken as a stream of 'transcendentally reduced' experiences) exists in an absolute sense, i.e. does not depend for its existence on anything external to itself. But if this is so, what role ontologically do the spatio-temporal things actually perform? The whole so-called 'natural world' could be merely a mirage, a nightmare dreamt by an excited mind. How real is my own body? How can I be sure of the existence of other minds independent of my own? The difficulty arising from regarding all existents as 'intentional objects of consciousness' is one of showing that there are existents which are not a creation of any consciousness.

Empirically, when we want to convince ourselves that a perceived object objectively exists we carry out certain tests. If I want to convince myself that this book in front of me is real and not imaginary I shall not confine myself to glancing at it a second time. The phenomenological distinction between the intentional object and the 'noematic content' of my act of perceiving it, alone, will tell me nothing about this object's existence 'external' to myself. Normally, I shall try and pick it up, open it, read it, perhaps consult other people and compare my experiences with theirs, etc. If I am in doubt about the existence of the chair which I can see opposite me across the table, one method of verification, although not nessessarily the least painful, is to try and sit on it. The choice of tests will depend on the nature of the object which I believe I see or expect to find in a certain place, on the criteria we adopt and on the amount of evidence required to satisfy these criteria.

These tests need not be conclusive, but the important thing is that they are undertaken on the assumption that there exists an 'external' spatio-temporal world. Husserl's *epoché* requires that we should *not* make such an assumption, but if we are not allowed to make such an assumption then it becomes difficult to explain the *meaning* of such tests. It becomes difficult to explain our treatment of empirical (spatio-temporal) objects generally.

The disturbing aspect of the reduction is that it has the effect of turning empirical objects into ontologically inferior entities compared with Husserl's 'general objects'. The crucial difference between these two kinds of objects, from Husserl's standpoint, is what Husserl calls their different 'modes of giveness' (giveness in a cognitive consciousness). An empirical object 'reveals' itself to us in series of aspects. These aspects change as the conditions of observation change, owing to such things as the object changing its position or the observer changing his, or to some other factor. An empirical object, as Husserl puts it, 'gives itself' in intuition, but only completely. This distinguishes empirical objects from the non-spatio-temporal 'general objects' (e.g. the species *red*) which, according to him, can be adequately apprehended in a 'categorial intuition'. Husserl differentiates accordingly between two kinds of 'self-evidence', or two kinds of what he calls 'self-giveness' of objects in intuition. Thus he speaks of 'assertoric' self-evidence and of 'apodeictic' self-evidence. The self-evidence of the fulfilment of a meaning-intention in the case of an empirical object would be of the former kind; the 'apodeictic self-evidence' is encountered only in the case of 'general objects'.

It should be pointed out that Husserl rejects the 'psychologistic' interpretation of self-evidence as a 'feeling of certainty' or 'feeling of obviousness'; to him 'self-evidence' is not a psychological but a phenomenological category; 'self-evidence' designates merely the fact of 'givenness' of the intended object in an act of identification. But since he distinguishes between *two kinds* of such givenness— between the assertoric and incomplete and the apodeictic and adequate—it would seem that objects falling into the latter class have a better claim to reality. The ontological status of an object would thus seem to be determined by the way in which this object can be 'given' in self-evidence to a 'transcendental consciousness'.

Transcendental solipsism

But one of the most serious consequences of the reduction is that by 'bracketing' the 'external world' and by transforming my own 'stream of experiences' into a stream of 'transcendentally reduced' experiences this reduction makes it difficult to show that there can in fact be different such streams of experiences; different consciousnesses and different egos. Husserl's problem in addition to numerous other difficulties caused by the phenomenological reduction was how to avoid the danger of a transcendental solipsism.

Husserl conceived the idea of a transcendental philosophy as based on a radical reduction in a period in which he was undergoing a deep intellectual crisis. With the first two volumes of *Logical Investigations* several years behind him and finding himself at forty-seven still unable to organise his ideas into what he would regard as a satisfactory 'philosophical system' his confidence seemed to desert him. He made his reputation with his devastating attack on psychologism and his phenomenological analysis of the epistemological foundations of logic. But he wanted to go further. He wanted to construct a more comprehensive system of philosophical explanation which would embrace all basic aspects of reality; but the vital clue to such a system seemed constantly to elude him.

It was in this situation that he turned to Kant for solace and inspiration. The idea of a transcendental phenomenological reduction which occurred to him during this time seemed to offer a solution to his problems. It seemed, at last, that a safe basis was found from which a systematic analysis of all philosophical problems could be successfully undertaken. Having overcome his earlier reservations about the transcendental approach, he now became convinced that a transcendental analysis based on the *epoché* was the only right road to take. His ultimate aim was to reconstitute the world as a transcendental system, but, as he soon discovered, there were certain fundamental difficulties in executing such a programme—even if we accept that the act of *epoché* on which such a programme depends is philosophically beyond reproach, which it is not. Thus it is highly questionable whether we can suspend all considerations of spatio-temporal existence and 'insulate' experiences from the world of the 'natural standpoint' as required by the *epoché*. But assuming that there are no objections to such an act of reduction, the risk that we are facing once we find ourselves transferred by the *epoché* into the region of so-called 'transcendental subjectivity', is that of losing contact with the real world, and, in view of the difficulty of showing that the act of *epoché* can be performed by different people at different times, of being forced into a solipsistic position with all the difficulties that this entails.

The main problem is this; how do I explain in transcendental-phenomenological terms the assumption that I make from my 'natural' ('non-philosophical') standpoint of the existence of an 'external world' and of other minds similar to my own? Unless I am able to do this I cannot claim to be able to reconstitute reality as a 'transcendental system'. This was the problem which Husserl faced and which he was never able to solve.

It is easy to see the difficulties that stand in the way of a 'phenomenological constitution'. Consider again the example of a book. I see a book lying in front of me on the table. The first distinction that I have to make is the distinction between the perception that I have of this book and the intentional object of my perception. But I can recognise this book as same in different perceptions. If, for example, I pick it up, change its position, open it, glance through its pages, put it away on a shelf, I have a whole series of perceptions, always being aware of having in front of me the same object. I can address myself to it in different meaning-giving acts, but there is something which persists in all these different acts and represents the principle of identification. Without it tests to verify the existence of the book would make no sense.

Husserl calls this identical something 'the pure X in abstraction from all predicates'. He also refers to it as the 'subject (*Sinnessubjekt*) of different essential types of meanings'. But the point is that this X represents the extra-mental thing which is ultimately responsible for verifying or falsifying the various 'noematic predicates' that are attached to it. In an epistemic context such an extra-mental thing can be given only 'problematically', that is as an object for *research*. In an act in which an object is 'problematically posited' it is also posited as transcendent with regard to what Husserl calls 'noema', and it is only because it is posited as transcendent that it makes sense to go and look for it in order to establish whether it in fact exists.

It is interesting to observe how the phenomenological status of such a 'problematically posited' object affects the phenomenological status of the ego. This object as the transcendent focus of various noematic predicates has apparently to be matched by an equally transcendent focus of the various subjective acts. At the transcendental level the two foci become the 'world' and the 'transcendental Ego'. But notice that both these foci remain of necessity 'transcendent' with regard to actual experiences. This being so it is difficult to see how the process of the so-called 'transcendental-phenomenological constitution' of the world can begin at all.

Husserl assures us that the concept of the 'transcendental Ego' is less abstruse than it may appear. According to Husserl, the position of the 'transcendental Ego' can be reached through a reflection upon my own empirical ego. By reflecting upon my own 'phenomenologically self-contained essence' as an individual person I become aware that this essence 'can be posited in an absolute sense, as I am the Ego who invests the being of the world which I so constantly speak about with existential validity, as an existence (*Sein*) which wins for me from my own life's pure essence meaning and substantiated validity. I myself as this individual essence, posited absolutely, as the open infinite field of pure phenomenological data and their inseparable unity, am the "transcendental Ego"; the absolute positing means that the world is no longer "given" to me in advance, its validity that of a simple existent, but that henceforth it is exclusively my Ego that is given (given from my new standpoint), given purely as that which has being in itself, in itself experiences a world, confirms the same, and so forth.'[1]

But this 'transcendental Ego' which I am supposed to discover through a reflection upon my own empirical self is clearly of a quite special kind. It is not a mere 'expansion' of my own ego; it is something entirely different for which, as Husserl himself points out, the word 'ego' itself *ceases to be suitable*. It is a *transcendental pole* correlated to that other pole called the *world*. But once this position has been reached, once I have 'bracketed' all empirical considerations the question is how do I explain, in transcendental terms, the 'possibility' of an empirical ego, my own ego, and its world? How can they be 'phenomenologically constituted' after they have been put in 'brackets'? How is it possible to constitute phenomenologically *other egos*? It is here that we face the danger of 'transcendental solipsism'.

It is true that Husserl made repeated efforts to overcome these difficulties and to show that his transcendental analysis does not lead to solipsistic conclusions.[2] But as his existentialist critics, among others, have shown, he never succeeded in proving that this in fact is not so. Husserl maintained that the experience of 'other egos' represents an essential and inseparable part of my own experience. But whilst one would not wish to dispute this view, it is far from clear how a phenomenological constitution of a 'polycentric inter-subjectivity' (the expression is Husserl's) can be effected once we have withdrawn to the position of the 'transcendental Ego'. Whatever Husserl may say in his own defence it is his transcendental *epoché* that cuts us off from the reality of 'other people'.

---

[1] See Husserl's Preface to the English translation of *Ideas* by W. R. Boyce Gibson (3rd imp., London, 1958) p. 17 ff.
[2] See especially *Cartesianische Meditationen* (Meditation V), *Husserliana*, vol.I.

8

THE CONCEPT OF LEBENSWELT

In the last years of his life Husserl made one final effort to show that his transcendental phenomenology is firmly rooted in historical reality and that the whole idea of 'phenomenological constitution' insofar as it draws attention to the *Leistung* of the human reason, has a profound humanist significance. He did this by critically analysing what he saw as the crisis of philosophically unenlightened science. The result was his last major work *The Crisis of European Sciences and Transcendental Phenomenology* of which the first two sections appeared in print in 1936, two years before Husserl's death, and the rest of the manuscript only posthumously.[1] The work remained unfinished.

That Husserl chose to defend his own position by subjecting modern science to critical scrutiny with a view to exposing its 'philosophical inadequacy', though significant, was not very surprising. We saw earlier that he based his transcendental analysis on the assumption that a true philosophical understanding of the world cannot come from the sciences of the 'natural standpoint'. One of the requirements of radical phenomenological reduction was that these sciences should be put in 'brackets', that we should make no use of their standards. Husserl was anxious to point out that a natural scientist *qua* natural scientist is not in a position to understand the meaning of his own work; he can do this only as a philosopher, and this requires 'putting out of action' the 'thesis of the natural standpoint' on which natural science rests. However, Husserl felt that he should define his attitude towards

[1] See *Husserliana*, vol. VI.

science in more precise terms. His views, he felt, were often misinterpreted and misunderstood. Certainly there was a growing hostility to transcendental phenomenology among scientifically minded philosophers. At the time when Husserl was trying to consolidate the results of his analysis and when the phenomenological school initiated by him began to view science with increasing suspicion—that is, in the years following the First World War—Logical Positivism with its emphasis on science was developing into a rival influence. Among the natural scientists and mathematicians at universities hostility to metaphysics rose in direct proportion to the diminishing interest in, and lack of understanding of, science among professional philosophers in the leading philosophy departments. The positivist movement was growing steadily, finding especially receptive ground in England. Its main exponent combined a strong empiricist conviction with an intense interest in the logico-linguistic problems of construction of scientific systems. Not surprisingly the movement found a large following among scientists of all denominations and tended to act as the official philosophical spokesman for science.

Having starter his own philosophical investigations with expressly scientific interests at heart, aiming at setting up a general theory of science, Husserl now saw his philosophy criticised and rejected as lacking in both scientific spirit and logical rigour. The hostility with which phenomenology was viewed in positivistic circles became even more intense after the irrationalist tendencies began gaining the upper hand within the phenomenological school. Phenomenology was attracting more and more men with the 'aesthetic' frame of mind who either did not understand science or were against what they considered to be its increasingly dangerous role in the life of society. The dangers of the technological age to modern Man were a popular subject of discussion. It was maintained that science, although not necessarily bad in itself, tends to divert Man's attention from the real issues of his existence and to obscure the values which Man should never lose sight of if he is not to lose himself as Man. And, so, while the positivistic movement was eulogising science and pouring scorn on the unscientific aberrations of metaphysicians, the phenomenological school was progressively turning away from science and seeking solutions in various brands of intuitionist metaphysics. The more the two schools grew in strength the deeper seemed to become the gulf between them. They developed and matured almost parallel with each other.[1] In 1927 Martin Heidegger,

[1] I am using here the term 'school' in a very loose sense to refer to the philosophers using similar methods, ignoring their individual differences which may of course be considerable.

the most distinguished and the most influential of Husserl's pupils, published his main work *Being and Time* (*Sein und Zeit*). In 1928, another outstanding phenomenologist, Max Scheler, published his celebrated essay on the 'Position of Man in the Cosmos' in which he defined Man not by his ability to do science but by his ability to acquire metaphysical knowledge. A year later the pupils and followers of Husserl's critic Moritz Schlick, gathered in the famous 'Vienna Circle', came out with their positivistic manifesto. The conflict between the two schools which had hitherto expressed itself in skirmishes between their respective exponents developed into a head-on clash between what amounted to two different ideologies, often with political implications.[1] The gulf between them became unbridgeable.

Husserl, of course, did not go as far as some of his pupils, although it has been said that towards the end of his life his thinking revealed traces of Heidegger's influence. But it is significant that his phenomenology became a source of inspiration to all those who distrusted science and that he himself eventually made an effort to expose what he regarded as the essential limitations of science and its inherent tendency to cloud the issues whose clarification, in his view, should be the main concern of philosophy.

However, the main driving force behind this attempt to expose the limitations of science, as we have already hinted, was the need to overcome the difficulties which had arisen within transcendental phenomenology itself. Husserl needed to clarify his own position in order to reassure himself as well as to reply to his critics. The idea of radical reduction seemed to create more difficulties than it was capable of solving. There was that excruciating problem of 'phenomenological constitution' of 'other egos' which kept cropping up. The charges of speculative sterility, lack of historical sense, obscurity and scientific irrelevance of his constructions, had to be answered. All this weighed on Husserl's mind when he began analysing what he regarded as the 'crisis of meaning' of modern science, trying at the same time to provide a new and, hopefully, more persuasive introduction to his own philosophy.

The crisis of meaning of science and scientific objectivism
But let us see what his basic objections against the attitudes based on or arising from science are. One of the main dangers, and a main

[1] The majority of the members and sympathisers of the 'Vienna Circle' tended to be cosmopolitan and socialist in their political outlook and many of them were driven abroad by the rising tide of Nazism, while some of the most influential phenomenologists were intensely nationalistic. Heidegger, as is well known, was for a time an active member of the Nazi Party.

source of crisis, in his view is the 'objectivistic physicalism' which permeates modern science. Husserl—this must be pointed out at once—is not against the 'physicalisation' of science as such; nor does he object to the progressive 'mathematisation of nature' which he himself regards as an inevitable result of the development of science as a whole. Nor is he against the scientific 'objectivism' as such. What he objects to is what he considers to be the false sense of *self-sufficiency* which this 'objectivism' tends to generate. Science, he emphasises, is not, and cannot be, self-sufficient. Science has progressed at a fantastic pace in modern times, but its progress has unleashed an intellectual crisis because science seems to have detached itself from the 'soil' from which it had originally sprung and from which alone it can receive a meaning. The 'crisis' of science is a crisis of its *meaning*. This, of course, does not affect its progress; science continues to make big advances. But, Husserl observes, our attitude towards science has become confused. We are not quite sure what role science plays, or should play, in human society; what its status is, what its obligations are, what it should mean to us human beings in the world in which we live. In the process of purifying the scientific criteria of all anthropocentric elements science has been literally de-humanised to the highest degree. New ideals of 'scientific truth' and 'scientific objectivity' have been created. The 'standpoint of subjectivity' with all its human implications has been swept aside by the tide of 'scientific objectivism'.

This development, according to Husserl, goes back to Galileo. It was Galileo who fathered the modern concept of the mathematised natural science. He aimed at achieving exactness and rational objectivity through *mathematisation*. Mathematisation meant the mathematical reconstruction of empirically observed processes. This involved inevitably a high degree of scientific *idealisation*. It involved a construction and detailed study of scientific models. The view became increasingly expressed that the main task of science was to penetrate through the thin layer of appearance to nature's mathematisable types. It was thought that all phenomena must be describable in terms of mathematical relations. The whole of nature came to be regarded as a kind of 'applied mathematics'. This prompted the platonist conclusion that the world as depicted in scientific idealisations was in fact the only real world. Consequently, science came to be regarded as the noblest and intellectually by far the most rewarding of occupations.

The idea of mathematisation of nature was coupled with the idea of universal causality. Galileo found that causal relationships can be mathematically expressed by means of formulae and this set the pattern for the scientific work in the centuries that followed. The

view that modern physics takes of causality may be different, but
—maintains Husserl—the Galilean ideal of a complete 'objectifi-
cation' of experience in a formalised language of science is still
very much alive. The aim of the scientist remains to translate
experience into impersonal formulae. He operates with models and
formulae and his job largely consists in constructing new models
and new formulae. While doing this he does not ask himself about
the historical presuppositions of his scientific work; still less does
he ask himself about the presuppositions of science in general.
He takes the 'trivialities' of the world in which he lives and works,
his own *Lebenswelt*, for granted. But the question is, can he really
afford to ignore the 'trivial truths' of his *Lebenswelt* if he wants to
understand the meaning of science? This is the problem that interests Husserl.

Since the days of Galileo's revolution mathematisation and
idealisation have become the main features of European science,
despite the differences between classical and present day physics
which remain considerable. Classical physics was a deterministic
physics; it based its methods on the assumption that every phenomenon has an unequivocally determinable place in the objective
mathematico-physical universe. The view of modern physics is that
univocity and exactness such as classical physics believed in cannot
be achieved. The modern physicist studies types, structures and
groups within which the behaviour of an individual can be pre-
dicted only with a lesser or greater degree of probability. The
concept of absolute calculability gives way to the concept of
probability and approximation to the calculable *type*. Modern
physics is in a special way concerned with the typical. It operates
with idealised models which function as probability types. It lays
emphasis on the importance of contextual determinations within
particular types.

But whether classical or modern, mathematico-physical idealisations, according to Husserl, are based on the same principle of
'scientific objectivism' which provoked the crisis of meaning mentioned earlier. They are idealisations in what is, in effect, a non-
human universe. The effect of the Galilean doctrine of scientific
objectivism was the gradual elimination of all specifically anthropocentric elements from science. This has greatly contributed towards
freeing science from historical prejudices but it has also blurred the
relation between science and man. Certain vital concepts such as
that of knowledge and truth have been scientifically reinterpreted
with the effect that they have practically lost what could be described
as their typically human content. Many philosophers have come to
accept as a matter of course the paradigmatic character of scientific

concepts and scientific methods. Scientific knowledge is regarded
as the paradigm of true knowledge. In the general enthusiasm for
science, the 'standpoint of subjectivity' is misunderstood, attacked
or simply ignored.

According to Husserl, philosophy can redress this situation by
focusing its attention on those 'trivial' truths of the *Lebenswelt*
—such as e.g. that I have a body, that I live in a community of
people, that a world exists, etc.—which are tacitly presupposed by
science and left unexplained. The general drive towards achieving
an ever greater degree of scientific 'objectivity' has had the effect
of obscuring the meaning of these simple truths. The *Lebenswelt* is
usually passed over and forgotten or else it is regarded as a source
of inaccuracies and imperfections in our language the sooner overcome the better. But the result of this, Husserl points out, is that
the real sense of scientific idealisation gets obscured. We tend to
forget or to overlook the link that connects these idealisations
with their historical background; the bewilderment about the
meaning of science is due to science being divorced from its historical
human context.

Husserl's criticism rests of course on purely philosophical considerations, but the time when he expressed it (1936) gave a special
meaning to his words, for the increasing abuse of dehumanised
science for political purposes was bringing nearer the disaster of
war which engulfed the world only a few years later.

Husserl's view was that modern science, although helping us to
understand nature better and to dominate it more successfully,
tends to conceal from us the world as *our* world. This was why he
referred to Galileo as the 'genius of discovery and concealment'.
The ideal which the scientist strives to achieve is the ideal of an
entirely impersonal objectivity. The scientist, quite properly, tries
to prevent any personal elements entering his descriptions and
affecting his experiments. He is always on the look out for objective
criteria which would reduce the ever-present possibility of error.
He avoids all references to himself if he can at all help it. He refuses
to accept untestable assumptions. His attitude is (or, at any rate
ought to be) one of completely unprejudiced objectivity. But whilst
all this helps him considerably in his work, it tends at the same
time to blind him to the historical sense of his constructions. He
tends to forget that his own life and the lives of others among whom
he lives, and a number of those 'trivial', 'matter of course' truths
which he accepts without questioning, form the historical basis of
all his constructions.

It is this basis which, according to Husserl, we must explore
phenomenologically if we want to make sense of science. The

position of science, according to him, can be fully understood only in the light of its 'non-scientific' presuppositions and these pre-suppositions are to be found in the domain of *Lebenswelt*. The *Lebenswelt* should therefore become the 'theme' of phenomenology.

The transcendental basis of Husserl's argument

The language in which Husserl's exhortations about the *Lebenswelt* are phrased is, however, somewhat misleading. Husserl's insistence on the 'historical context' might suggest that he has abandoned his transcendental position in favour of a historical analysis. Nothing could be further from the truth. We shall see this clearly if we analyse the concept of *Lebenswelt* a little more closely.

We are asked by Husserl to concentrate our attention on the 'trivial' truths of the 'world in which we live'. But this world is changing, historical conditions are changing, people are changing their habits, and their views. Different people in different parts of the world have different views of life and hold different opinions on what the highest priorities and values are. Where are we to begin our analysis? How can we escape relativism? We can do this, Husserl assures us, because the *Lebenswelt* in all its relativities has a general structure; it has certain permanent features which are always there and we can escape relativism by focusing our attention on these features.

But what are these features and how do we discover them and describe them? How can we establish the alleged invariant structure of the *Lebenswelt* and explain its significance? It soon became clear that Husserl could approach an answer to these questions only at the level of his transcendental analysis and this gave his talk about *Lebenswelt* as the 'historical basis' merely a metaphorical significance. The gulf between the historical and the transcendental standpoint remained as deep as ever. *Lebenswelt* was a philosophical not a historical category. The so-called 'trivial' truths of *Lebenswelt* were subject to 'phenomenological constitution'. In other words, they had to be explained in *a priori* transcendental terms, and this meant returning to the transcendental Ego and all the problems and difficulties connected with it.

Husserl indeed continued to insist on the necessity of the radical phenomenological reduction. He contrasted the 'Galilean objecti-vism' with Descartes' discovery of subjectivity and while taking, generally, the Cartesian line of approach he continued to criticise what he regarded as the 'incompleteness' of the 'Cartesian reduction'. Descartes maintained that in order to discover a genuine beginning in philosophy everything should be provisionally subjected to doubt, in which case we shall be rewarded with the indubitable truth of *ego cogito*. But, in Husserl's view, Descartes misinterpreted his own achievement, for he confused the *ego* with a substantival self instead of regarding it as the transcendental Ego-pole correlated to the world. It was not quite clear to Descartes that Ego was not *an* ego, but *the Ego*, the one and only basis of the transcendental phenomenological constitution. If he had clearly understood the essence of the Ego—Husserl says—he would have understood the need and the importance of such a constitution. He would have understood that distinctions such as between I and You, internal and external are to be constituted in the 'Absolute Ego'.[1]

But against the background of such radical transcendentalism the exhortations about the importance of the historical *Lebenswelt* sound pretty hollow. Husserl reproached scientifically minded philosophers for 'forgetting' the *Lebenswelt*, but since from his standpoint the basic truths of the *Lebenswelt* can be explained only through the 'Aboslute Ego', his reproaches to these philosophers amounted to saying that they 'forgot' to concern themselves with the 'Absolute Ego' and this is an objection which can hardly carry much weight.

The truth is that Husserl himself was at a loss how to bridge the gap between the 'Absolute Ego' and the reality of the historical *Lebenswelt*. As a result of the transcendental reduction he reached the position of a 'peculiar philosophical insularity' which he claimed to be a 'methodical precondition' of a truly radical philosophy, but which made it extremely difficult for him to explain the real world around him. One of the most difficult problems he faced, as we have already pointed out, was that of explaining the possibility of 'other egos', other subjects, who presumably are equally capable of reaching that peculiar transcendental level at which he conducted his analysis. Clearly, in order to solve this problem it is necessary to break the 'peculiar philosophical insularity' of the 'Absolute Ego'. But how can this be done? How can Husserl overcome his own insularity without at the same time abandoning his method? His attempts at a 'phenomenological constitution of intersubjectivity' yielded little more than feeble and unpersuasive psychological analogies. Thus he looked, among other things, to 'acts of memory' in his search for a clue to 'other egos'. In an act of memory, he says, in which I re-construct a past experience I constitute my ego in a different modus; I think not of my present I but of my past I; I think of my I in the 'past modus' and in doing so I transcend, in a sense, the presence of my own ego. In a similar way, he maintains, the 'transcendental Ego' can constitute another ego in an act of 'self-transcendence'. But all this only exposes the precariousness of Husserl's own position,

[1] cf. *Husserliana*, vol. VI, p. 84.

for it is clear that on the basis of the suggested analogy I can think of 'other egos' only as modifications of my own ego and not at all as something independent of myself. I cannot show the possibility of *genuinely* other egos in this way. Another suggestion by Husserl was that a phenomenological analysis of empathy might provide a solution to the problem. But while it is clear that through empathy and fellow-feeling we can 'detect' other egos, the question is how can the possibility of their existence be explained in *transcendental* terms, for this is what Husserl's method requires.

Husserl's preoccupation with *Lebenswelt* was not merely an expression of his desire to expose the philosophical inadequacy of 'scientific objectivism'; it was also an indication that he became uneasily aware of the deficiencies of his own transcendental analysis. He wanted to eliminate these deficiencies, but this could have been achieved only by abandoning large portions of his doctrine and he was never prepared to go this far.

If we glance back at Husserl's philosophical development from his *Philosophy of Arithmetic* onward, we shall see that, at root, all his analyses were concerned with one basic problem: the problem of the relation between the objective content of knowledge and the acts of meaning and knowing. Or, to repeat one of his own questions: 'How are we to understand the fact that the "in-itself" of the objectivity can be thought of by us and moreover "apprehended" in cognition, and thus in the end yet become "subjective"?' It was this problem that led the young mathematician Husserl to interest himself in the noetic presuppositions of mathematics and to inquire into the 'origin' of the concept of number. He was made aware by Brentano of the importance of intentional relations, and in exploring these relations he found himself in the domain of that 'object-constituting subjectivity' (*die leistende Subjektivität*, as he came to call it) which was to remain the focal point of his phenomenological analyses.

The conceptual analysis and the method of definitions, Husserl felt, useful though they are within certain contexts, are philosophically insufficient and often inapplicable. We need a descriptive phenomenological method to complement them. Logicians, as a rule, tend to ignore the fact that there is a 'subjective' as well as an 'objective' aspect to meaning, that we must analyse the 'phenomenon of meaning' in its entirety, that is, not merely from the aspect of the 'meant as such' but also from the aspect of the act of meaning which is an intentional act. Logical objects—concepts, propositions, etc.— are not just a special class of items with which we happen to be concerned and which can be analysed, defined, explained, in terms

of other similar or non-similar items; they involve *acts* and they must
be studied in conjunction with these acts with which they are
structurally connected.

Husserl's point was that in order to clarify the pre-suppositions
of logic we must undertake a phenomenological analysis of 'experiences of meaning'. This was precisely what he did—his analysis of
the presuppositions of logic, as we saw, gradually expanding into an
analysis of the presuppositions of knowledge in general. It was
along this road that he finally arrived at the transcendental position
of his later years. He wanted to show that the world, the totality
of facts, is structurally dependent on, and inseparable from, an
intentional object-constituting *consciousness*. But in this he failed.
In order to succeed he would have had to prove that a programme of
transcendental phenomenological constitution of the world can
indeed be successfully carried out but he was never able to provide
such a proof.

Husserl's difficulties were due largely to his radical transcendentalism. He conducted his analysis from the standpoint of the 'trans-
dendental subjectivity'. He used the adjective 'transcendental' in
order to underline that this subjectivity was neither psychological
nor 'existential' (in the sense given to it by the existentialist philosophers) nor subjectivistic. Of course, one cannot but begin within
one's own 'stream of experiences', within one's own subjectivity.
But, according to Husserl, the radical *epoché* transforms this subjectivity into a transcendental subjectivity, a sphere of transcendental
facts about knowledge *in general*. This is, among other things, why
he does not wish to see this subjectivity interpreted in purely anthropological terms (although, naturally enough, he regards his own
analysis as directly relevant to, and necessarily presupposed by, a
philosophical anthropology). He is first and foremost a transcendental philosopher, not a philosophical anthropologist. We shall
see that the existential phenomenologists too do not regard their
own analyses as falling under the heading of philosophical anthropology. But that there exists a close connection between the adoption
of the phenomenological method as basic and certain anthropological assumptions will be seen clearly if we examine the views of
Max Scheler.

9

SCHELER'S ANTHROPOLOGY

After Husserl, Max Scheler was one of the most productive and, at the same time, one of the most original minds in the 'phenomenological school'. The perspicacity of his observations, his wealth of ideas, the lively sense of language and a degree of clarity which neither Husserl nor Heidegger were able to achieve—all these combined to give to his writings an attraction which even his opponents rarely failed to acknowledge. He applied the phenomenological method to a field which remained largely outside Husserl's sphere of interest, the field of the emotions. Scheler was attracted by the problem of values and in his main ethical work *Formalism in Ethics and the Material Ethics of Values* (1916) he tried to develop an ethic of values on the basis of a phenomenological analysis of the emotional 'acts of preferring'. He attacked Kant's 'ethical formalism' which seemed to legislate, so to speak, from above, completely disregarding the nature of concrete preferential acts. The assumption underlying Kant's attitude was that every 'material' (i.e. non-formal) ethic is necessarily empiricist and degenerates into forms of hedonism and utilitarianism. Contrary to this, Scheler wanted to show that a 'material ethic of values' need not be either empiricist or materialistic; it can be *a priori*, and this is so because there is an 'objective hierarchy of ideal values' which can be phenomenologically analysed and described. These hierarchically ordered values, according to Scheler, form an independent region of 'ideal objects'. Unlike Husserl's 'ideal objects', Scheler's 'ideal objects' had a much more pronounced platonist flavour.

Scheler's quarrel with Kant was not about the *possibility* of an *a priori* analysis but about the *nature* of such an analysis and about Kant's apparent inability to understand the role of emotions. 'What we insist upon . . . in opposition to Kant'—Scheler writes—'is the *a priori* of the emotional and we demand that a distinction be drawn between the *a priori* method and rationalism, which hitherto have been falsely assumed to be inseparable. It is not at all necessary for an "emotional" as distinct from a "rational" ethic to be "empiricist" in the sense of trying to define moral values on the basis of observation and induction. Acts of feeling, preference and disapprobation, love and hate, have an *a priori* content which is just as independent of the inductive experience as are the pure laws of thought. In either case an essential intuition (*Wesensschau*) is possible of acts and their contents, their foundation and their mutual connections. In either case there is a self-evidence and the strictest exactness in the phenomenological description of facts.'[1]

Kant mistrusted emotions. Emotional preferences, in his view, all too frequently lead to confusion and conflict in moral appraisal. Kant did not think that a consistent ethical theory could be based on an analysis of emotional acts, let alone an *a priori* ethic. He reasoned, roughly, in the following way. If, for example, I save someone's life because I expect to be rewarded or because I like jumping into cold water, or because I happen to love the person involved, my action, strictly speaking, cannot be described as a 'moral' action because it is motivated by self-interest. If an action is to have moral worth it must be done from a sense of duty, that is, out of respect for the moral law. An action cannot be called a moral action if the person who performs it does so because of the benefits that might accrue to him as a result of it. It is only when he acts from a sense of duty and for the sake of the moral law that moral value attaches to his action. Of course, it is quite possible that a moral action may bring material benefits to the one who performs it, or increase his personal happiness and the happiness of others, but what makes it 'moral', according to Kant, is not that it brings material or other advantages but solely the fact that it is done out of respect for the moral law.

Scheler agrees that utilitarian considerations should not play a part in deciding the morality of an action, but he at the same time strongly opposes the view that emotions could be bypassed in examining the foundations of ethics. There can be no question of bypassing or 'suppressing' emotions because it is precisely through emotional acts that we detect values, and therefore also ethical values. This, Scheler emphasises, does not mean that an ethic of

[1] Max Scheler, *Der Formalismus in der Ethik und die materiale Wertethik* (Berlin, 1954), p. 85 ff.

values must be hedonist or utilitarian or relativistic. There are certain values which are eternal and unchangeable, and the task of a phenomenological analysis of 'acts of preferring' is precisely to determine and order these values. The highest values, according to Scheler, are discovered in acts of love. To Kant's ethics of 'dry duty' Scheler contrasts his own ethics of *love*.

But if we want to find a real clue to Scheler's general philosophical position, we must turn to his anthropology. The question as to what place anthropological problems should occupy in phenomenological investigations is a matter of dispute. But there is no doubt that both Scheler's ethics of love and the metaphysics of knowledge which he developed in his later years are more readily understood if one is familiar with his view of Man.

Scheler, as we already hinted, widened the area of phenomenological analysis beyond the sphere of what is sometimes called 'intellectual acts' to embrace the vast domain of the *irrational*. Husserl based his inquiry on the idea of the Ego as a transcendental pole correlated to what he called the 'world'. Scheler based his investigations on the idea of a *person* as a centre not only of 'intellectual' but also of volitional and emotional acts.

This widening of the basis of the phenomenological inquiry seemed to have many important advantages. One of them was the apparently easier access to the area of intersubjectivity which so doggedly eluded Husserl. We saw that Husserl found it extremely difficult to 'constitute' 'other egos' on his premisses. Scheler's approach seemed to hold out the promise of overcoming the 'intellectual insularity' of the Ego and of making the 'world of others' readily accessible. Husserl had to struggle against the ghost of transcendental solipsism. Scheler seemed to have managed to escape solipsism by recognising the value of 'extra-rational' acts and by showing that the 'others' can be found at this 'extra-rational', emotional level. His lead in this was followed by the existentialists who were even more anxious to avoid Husserl's 'intellectualism'. If we abandon the 'intellectualist' attitude, the existentialists argue, the so-called problem of 'other egos' will cease to exist. In any case, it is wrong to ask how I can 'prove' that there can be other minds similar to my own. I live with other people, work with them, talk to them; I am in a continuous relationship with them. The essence of my being is being-with-others, or, as Sartre would say, *being-for-others*. Without 'others' I would not be what I am. My experience, in communication, of a *you* external to myself is a confirmation of my own existence. It is through an active relationship with other people that I become aware of the nature of my own individual self. Scheler expressed this succinctly by saying that there is 'no *I* without *we*'. Self-consciousness is not something that can be entirely dissociated from social consciousness. Self-observation (*Selbstbetrachtung*)—says Scheler—always begins as an observation of one's own self 'as if' one were someone else.[1] The idea of 'the other', 'the thou' is an integral part of the consciousness that we have of ourselves.

What is important to bear in mind is that this 'other' is not an object, but a being similar to myself. One of the main objections that both Scheler and the existentialists raised against Husserl was precisely that from a purely intellectualist position 'the other' cannot be construed otherwise than as an *object*. If we want to discover 'the other' at our own level, they say, we must concentrate on the analysis not of purely epistemic 'intellectual' acts but of emotional acts such as can be found in our actual relationship with other people. We must analyse 'social emotions' which reveal directly the presence of other beings similar to ourselves, such as *love, sympathy* and *shame*.

'Technical intelligence' and the essence of man

The problem of 'other people' had the curious effect of strengthening the anti-rationalist tendencies in the 'phenomenological school'. It opened, it seemed, yet another area of philosophical truth lying beyond the reach of rationalising reflection and objectifying science in general. As a result, the interest in science among phenomenologists diminished still further.

We saw that Husserl tried to expose what he regarded as the philosophical inadequacy of the standpoint of natural science. Scheler tried to do the same in the context of a philosophical anthropology. Scheler's thesis was that scientific knowledge is not the highest type of knowledge of which Man is capable. What makes Man the kind of being he is, Scheler maintained, is not his ability to do science. This ability is certainly not something that distinguishes him radically from animals. Between Edison and an intelligent chimpanzee, so long as the former is regarded purely as a 'technician', there is, Scheler says, only a difference in *degree*, however considerable this difference may be. It is only when Edison is looked upon as someone who is capable not only of scientific knowledge but also of *a priori* metaphysical knowledge that the fundamental difference between them becomes apparent. Man's distinguishing characteristic, according to Scheler, consists in his being able to acquire metaphysical knowledge about himself and his own position in the universe; it consists in his having privileged access to that region of 'essences' of which Husserl spoke and which was now widened by Scheler to include the hierarchy of values

[1] cf. *Die Wissensformen und die Gesellschaft* (Bern, 1960), p. 374.

discovered through a phenomenological analysis of 'emotional acts'.

As to *how* do we discover these essences, Scheler's answer to this question is again reminiscent of Husserl: through *acts of ideation*. An act of ideation, Scheler explains, is entirely different from anything that comes under the headings of 'technical intelligence' and 'deductive thinking'. A problem for 'technical intelligence', according to Scheler, would be the following: 'I now have a pain in my arm —how did this pain develop and how can it be eliminated? This is a task for positive science, for physiology, psychology, medicine. But'—he goes on—'I can assume a more detached, reflective, contemplative attitude and look at this same pain as an "example" illustrating the most peculiar and the most astonishing fact (*Wesensverhalt*) that in this world there are things such as pain, evil and suffering; I shall then phrase my question differently, and ask: What is *pain as such*—quite irrespective of my feeling pain here and now—and what must the ultimate principle of things be like for something like pain to be at all possible?'[1] It is only when we assume such a contemplative attitude, claims Scheler, that we become able to reach beyond the immediate facticity of a phenomenon to the essence which this phenomenon exemplifies. Just like Husserl, Scheler speaks of the conversion of things into *examples* as a fundamental characteristic of an act of ideation. An act of ideation is an intentional act in which we discover essences in the form of meanings and values.

It is through these acts that, according to Scheler, Man asserts specific qualities which distinguish him from the rest of the animal world. It is because he is able to extricate himself from the material context in which he lives, to raise himself above the immediate exigencies of life and to acquire knowledge of essences, that he enjoys a special position in the universe. We shall be able to see more clearly what all this implies if we examine Scheler's conception of 'life' in some detail.

Forms of life

Scheler distinguishes four basic strata or forms of life. The lowest form is represented by the blind organic drive which he calls *Gefühlsdrang*. This drive is a drive towards growth and reproduction and is shared by all living things. The best illustration of it as a primitive form of life is to be found in the life of plants. A plant, in fact, has little else apart from this general life drive. It has no sense organs, no nervous system, no ability to learn or to remember. It has no motorial centres and no limbs, it cannot move about as an animal can. It is confined to the small patch of soil from which it grows

[1] *Die Stellung des Menschen im Kosmos* (Francke Verlag, Bern und München, 1962), pp. 49 ff.

D

and from which it extracts all its food. In animals and humans the organic drive is combined with higher forms of life, but its general function remains the same. Its special importance—according to Scheler—lies in the fact that it acts as the vehicle of that original experience of *resistance* without which there would be no experience of *reality*. Reality, maintains Scheler, reveals itself through resistance and this resistance is originally experienced in the organic drive.

The second stratum or form of life, according to Scheler, is represented by *instinct*. With instinct we find ourselves already in the animal world. Instinct represents an 'increasing specialisation of the organic drive and its qualities'. It manifests itself in a purposive behaviour which gives the impression of the animal having an advance knowledge of a certain state of affairs. Instinct, however, is not something peculiar to an individual animal, but represents a feature characteristic of the species as a whole. As to how it is acquired, Scheler's view is that it cannot be explained simply as a result of a long process of learning on the basis of conditioned reflexes by successive generations of a species, but that it must be considered in the context of the general organic constitution of the given species. It is the organic constitution of the species that determines the nature of the instinct and, according to Scheler, this explains why instinct goes deeper than the 'knowledge' accumulated through learning by association. In instinctive behaviour the animal reveals in a special way the close ties that bind him to the species. By acquiring the ability of learning through what Scheler calls the 'associative memory', on the other hand, the animal becomes capable of a greater individual independence.

Scheler consequently regards the 'associative memory' as a higher form of life. The basis of associative memory is the conditioned reflex. Pavlov's famous experiments with dogs give an illustration of how conditioned reflexes operate. A signal associated with a meal will cause a dog to secrete an extra amount of saliva in the expectation of food. By the same principle of association, a mouse will learn, after a number of trials, to avoid blind alleys and find the way out of a maze. Successful training of animals entirely depends on the establishing of the right kind of conditioned reflexes. The process of learning and accumulating experience on the basis of conditioned reflexes results in an increased capacity for adaptation to changed conditions. This represents an enormous progress compared with the 'rigidity' of instinct. But, according to Scheler, this is by no means the highest form of mental activity of which animals are capable.

There is a *fourth* form of life which Scheler calls 'practical intelli-gence' and which includes the ability to choose between different things or courses of action. This too can be found in the animal world. The difference between intelligent behaviour and behaviour based on conditioned reflexes is that the latter depends on the repetition of the same signal or the same situation, whereas the former involves a flexible response to changed circumstances and the ability to find solutions to new problems. The well known experiments with anthropoid monkeys have shown that the latter possess this kind of intelligence. A chimpanzee will find a way of piling up empty boxes thrown into his cage so that he can climb on to them and get the fruit suspended from the top; or, as Köhler's experiments showed, he will eventually find out how to fit two hollow sticks into each other in order to reach the banana lying outside the cage.

However, although animals undoubtedly possess practical intelligence there is—Scheler maintains—still an enormous gulf that divides them from Man. This is not merely because Man has *more* intelligence; the difference between man and animals is not one of degree: it is a *fundamental* difference. In addition to practical intelligence, Man—claims Scheler—possesses something that does not come under the broad heading of 'life'. 'The principle which makes Man the kind of being he is'—he writes—'does not represent a new stage of life . . . it is a principle which stands in opposition to all life, even to the life in Man.'[1] This new principle he calls *Spirit* (*Geist*).

Man—the 'ascetic of life'

Scheler's contrasting of *Spirit* with Life in the above quotation is somewhat confusing. What he wants to say, briefly, is this: it is through *Spirit* that Man asserts his ability to detach himself from the organic and environmental context which the animal practically never leaves. The being which has *Spirit* has the ability to raise himself to a level from which it can neutralise, as it were, the sources of resistance and contemplate them as ideal objects. The animal is not capable of this. It lives within its own environment without being able to detach itself from it and contemplate it as an object. It carries its environment with it, Scheler says, as the snail carries its house. It cannot 'withdraw' from its environment and look at it from a distance. It is completely absorbed in life. It is true that the animal possesses intelligence. But this intelligence is a 'practical intelligence' geared to the practical needs of the animal, its sole task being to find the means of satisfying these needs. Unlike Man the animal is not capable of an act of ideation which involves an act of withdrawal from the immediate reality of things and a funda-

[1] ibid., p. 37.

mental change of attitude leading to the discovery of ideal 'essences'.

It is now clear why Scheler does not regard scientific knowledge as the highest form of knowledge. His view is that natural science represents only an expansion of that practical intelligence which can already be found among higher apes. Man, he believes, is capable of a higher form of knowledge—the knowledge acquired through acts of ideation, through that Cartesian act of withdrawal from the immediate spatio-temporal context to which Husserl gave the name 'phenomenological reduction'. To Scheler, 'phenomenological reduction' is a highly significant anthropological phenomenon. It is something that distinguishes Man from the rest of the animal world as a creature endowed with *Spirit*.

The act of *ideation* and the act of *reduction*, Scheler points out, go hand in hand. It is impossible to 'apprehend' an 'ideal object', an 'essence', through an act of ideation without at the same time performing an 'act of reduction', i.e. without setting aside for the time being the existential *here-now-thus* aspect of the empirical object at which our act of ideation is directed. In this Scheler is in basic agreement with Husserl. The reduction inevitably involves a suspension of spatio-temporal existential considerations. What Scheler does *not* accept is Husserl's interpretation of this act of reduction as an act of 'bracketing' of existential *judgements*. The reduction, maintains Scheler, involves much more than this. It involves a tentative suspension not merely of existential judgements but of the existential aspect *as such*. It involves an act of withdrawal from the position from which we discover the reality of things through resistance. It is, Scheler says, an 'ascetic act'; an act by which the life-drive as the subject of the experience of resistance is, as it were, put out of action in order to make room for *Spirit*. To Scheler, then, the reduction is not merely an intellectual exercise which makes it possible for us to reinterpret the world from a different angle. It is something much more important: it is a self-assertion of *Spirit* in Man and an act in which Man discovers his own innermost essence. Whereas for Husserl the reduction, in its radical application, leads to the discovery of the 'transcendental Ego', for Scheler it leads to the discovery of the *person* as the centre of *Spirit*.

It is through the reduction, says Scheler, through the 'ascetic acts' of suppression of the life-drive, through acts of ideation in which Man discovers ideal values, that he asserts himself as someone who is more than just an intelligent animal. Man, Scheler says, is the being who can say 'no'. He is the 'ascetic of life'. Through his 'no' to the physical immediacy of things—in other words, through the reduction—he is able to raise himself to a higher level and contemplate the world as someone who can 'detach himself from it'. In acts of ideation which are an expression of this 'no', man is able to *transcend* the context of spatio-temporal experience and acquire a knowledge which ranks higher than the knowledge based on natural science. Unlike scientific knowledge, this knowledge—says Scheler— is based on *a priori* insights into essences, and what is recognised as valid as a result of such insights is valid not only in this world but in 'all possible worlds'. It is as someone capable of such *a priori* insights that Man asserts himself as the centre of *Spirit*.

Scheler uses here his anthropology as a spring-board for far-reaching metaphysical construction which display his characteristic imagination and ingenuity but which are, for all their poetic splendour, philosophically of small value. All we need say about these constructions is that they took the form of a pantheistic metaphysics with *Spirit* and Life-Drive becoming the two attributes of the Absolute. According to Scheler, *Spirit* as such is weak and powerless and it can act only through the forces of Life. There is a constant tension between the two, yet it is only through the process of their progressive mutual permeation that the Absolute 'reveals' itself. Scheler sees Man as the scene of this process. It is through Man, through the acts by which he reveals the ideal values and guides the blind Life-Drive towards the achievement of these values, that, according to Scheler, the Absolute realises and asserts itself.

However, what interests us here are the basic anthropological assumptions underlying Scheler's analysis and these assumptions can be briefly summed up thus. Man is a being who can 'withdraw' from the spatio-temporal world into himself and in this very act of 'withdrawal' he rediscovers the world as an object. He can 'stand back' and contemplate the world and himself with a detached mind, and only because he can do this is he able to see clearly what is essentially involved in what the existentialists call his being-in-the-world. Man can transcend the world of spatio-temporal existence, he can say 'no', and this is the foundation of his freedom. Man is free not merely because he is able to 'make choices', but because he can extricate himself from the spatio-temporal context and recognise the contingency of everything existent. All this is implicitly contained in the contention that Man is capable of intuiting essences through acts of ideation, which is one of the basic tenets of phenomenology. Phenomenologists, as a rule, do not wish to be called anthropologists, and we shall see that Heidegger, among others, rejects any suggestion that his philosophy might be resting on certain anthropological presuppositions and insists that his primary concern in any case is with *being* and not specifically with Man. But it is nevertheless true that the assumptions mentioned above remain a guiding light of all his analyses.

IN SEARCH OF THE MEANING OF 'BEING'

Max Scheler endeavoured to show that the fundamental difference which divides men from animals and secures for Man a special position in the world lies ultimately in Man's ability to acquire a knowledge which lies beyond the reach of mere 'technical intelligence'. Furthermore, only Man is able to raise himself to a level from which he can contemplate the world of which he himself is a part as an object—and hence contemplate the possibility of the world not existing at all. These are essential characteristics of Man's own distinctive manner-of-being. However, all too often these characteristics are overlooked or ignored and, as a result, a distorted picture is given of the nature of Man. An example of such a distortion, from Scheler's point of view, is the view of Man as *homo faber*.

Man, according to Scheler, is not merely a 'faber'—someone who is able to use tools to some purpose, produce goods, make things, utilise the sources of energy available in nature and generally transform his environment. Man is also someone who is able to rise above his own 'productive activity' and look at what he is doing, as it were, from a distance. He is someone who tries to *understand* the world and himself. He is the 'centre of understanding'. An essential feature of Man's own manner-of-being is his ability to 'give meaning' and to 'make sense'. Husserl and Scheler are in agreement on this. For them the *homo faber* view is closely connected with the 'standpoint of natural science', so that the criticism directed against the former inevitably hits the latter as well. It is therefore not surprising that whilst beginning their analyses from somewhat different premisses, Husserl and Scheler arrived, with regard to science, at very similar conclusions.

They were, of course, not against science as such, but they were firmly convinced that science is incapable of penetrating the precincts of *Spirit* proper. Consequently, they maintained that it is useless to try and gain an adequate *philosophical* understanding of ourselves and the world through science. This view began to be expressed more and more frequently in phenomenological circles. The more the modern enthusiasm for science spread, the stronger the opposition of the phenomenologists to science-oriented philosophy seemed to become. They were concerned about *Spirit* and values and feared science as a possible destroyer of both. Eventually, this fear and increasing concern about the fate of the individual in the modern technological age induced a feeling of aversion for science which the phenomenological philosophers of existence no longer attempted to hide. They came to regard science as something which positively blocks the way towards a true understanding of human existence.

The attitude of *Martin Heidegger* in this respect is very revealing. His view of modern science is that of a 'technical, practical business of gaining and transmitting information' in which the practical intelligence triumphs but the effect of which is a perilous suppression of *Spirit*. (The word *Spirit* is the nearest here although not an entirely satisfactory translation of the German word 'Geist' which has a wider meaning than its English counterpart has in ordinary speech.) Heidegger claims that the growing popularity and the growing dominance of science in the societies of both East and West have been accompanied at the social-political level by the rising influence of mediocrity and the general self-assertion of the average man. Metaphysically speaking—he says in his *Introduction to Metaphysics* which contains the lectures delivered by him in 1935 and published after the war—there is no difference between Russia and America; on both sides we find the 'same dreary frenzy of unleashed technology and rootless organisation of the average man'.[1] Heidegger sees in this a sign of a general 'spiritual decline'. There is a tendency to confuse *Spirit* with 'intelligence', to downgrade *Spirit* and reduce it to something from which it is manifestly different. This situation, according to Heidegger, is faithfully reflected in the two philosophies which have become the leading ideologies of the two worlds: *Marxism* and *Positivism*. Heidegger sees both Marxism and Positivism as a manifestation of 'intelligence' and as essentially hostile to the cause of *Spirit*. According to him, they are products of a technocratic age in which *Spirit* is threatened by the rising tide of 'scientific intelligence' and 'social mediocrity'. It is essential, thinks Heidegger, that this process

[1] *Einführung in die Metaphysik* (Tübingen, 1935), p. 28.

of spiritual degeneration should be halted, and in his view it is
Europe, and in particular Germany, that should reassert themselves
as a guardian of *Spirit*. It hardly needs saying that Heidegger regards
his own philosophy as a necessary basis for any such act of re-
assertion.

Max Scheler was the one who by his distinction between 'technical
intelligence' and '*Spirit*' formulated very clearly the presupposition
of such a philosophical attitude, although his anthropological
approach is regarded by other phenomenologists with some dis-
favour. As pointed out earlier, phenomenologists as a rule do not
wish to be classed as 'philosophical anthropologists'. This applies
to both the 'transcendental' and the 'existential' phenomenologists.
They maintain that their primary aim is not to define the 'essence
of man' but to describe what they call the 'basic phenomenologica.
facts'. The 'phenomenological facts', they all insist, must come first.
We saw that Husserl studiously avoided all purely anthropological
considerations in his analysis, although all the signs pointed in the
direction of man. Heidegger is equally if not even more determined
to eliminate every suggestion of an anthropology from his own
analysis. The main object of his interest is *being*, and he consequently
describes his inquiry as a phenomenological ontology. The first and
foremost philosophical task, in his view, is the clarification of the
meaning of *being*. If the assertion that man enjoys a special position
in the universe is to have any sense, then this assertion must be based
on an analysis of the meaning of *being*, or, more precisely, on an
analysis of the *understanding* that man has or can have of *being*.
An anthropology must have *ontological* foundations. Heidegger's
warnings about the dangers to *Spirit* are motivated exclusively by his
concern about *being* and by his belief that the 'horizon of understanding' of *being* becomes inevitably obscured in the domain of
'technical intelligence'. Let us, then, see how he approaches the
task of clarifying the meaning of *being* and what basic presuppositions underlie his analysis.

The words 'being' and 'to be'

First, a few preliminary explanations. The word 'being' is notor-
iously equivocal and this presents a considerable difficulty. Grammatically, it unites the qualities of present participle, gerund, verbal
substantive and simple noun. In different contexts it may mean very
different things. What is important above all is not to lose sight
of its origin. 'Being' is a derivative of 'to be' and it is the meaning
of this 'existential' verb that should be considered first. The connexion
between 'being' and 'to be' is more directly conveyed by the German
das Sein which is obtained by simply prefixing the definite article

to the infinitive. The same applies to the French word *l'Etre* and to the Italian *il Essere*.

In Heidegger's philosophy many important terms are derived from *sein* and it is not always easy to find adequate translations for them. One of them is '*Dasein*' which in his ontology stands for Man and which readily reveals a connexion with *sein* but is impossible to translate so as to preserve this important connexion, unless we are prepared to use ugly constructions. Another term which causes some difficulty is *das Seiende*. This term designates any existent thing, including humans. Some translators reproduce it by the plural 'beings' to distinguish it from 'being' which is reserved for *das Sein*. But the word 'beings' apart from creating a difficult situation when we want to refer to an individual *Seiendes* suggests *live* beings, whereas '*das Seiende*' designates absolutely anything that can be said to exist. This is why the word 'existent' is often used. This too has its disadvantages because the word 'existent' is too close to 'existence' which is in Heidegger's philosophy a very special category reserved exclusively for the *Dasein*'s (=Man's) own distinct manner-of-being. However, in the absence of a better word we shall use the word 'existent', replacing it occasionally by the word 'thing', depending upon the context.

But let us turn our attention to 'to be'. What is its meaning and where is this meaning rooted? Compared with other verbs 'to be' shows an exceptional variety of inflected forms: *am, is, are, was, were,* etc. Among these 'is' is often given a privileged position—for example, in logic. In fact, it is through 'is' that we generally tend to explain the infinitive 'to be'. But, Heidegger points out, 'is' occurs in many different contexts and conveys many different meanings. We say, 'The rose *is* red', 'The conference *is* in the Memorial Hall', 'He *is* from Newcastle', 'That book *is* mine', 'There *is* a fireplace in this room', 'The number two *is* the first prime', 'What *is* to be done?', 'It *is* raining', etc. 'Is' can be used to attribute a property, to assert existence, to express identity and in so many other meanings. What do all these different applications of 'is' have in common? It is difficult to see how we can on this basis reach a clear definition of 'to be'. But are we to conclude from this that 'to be' and its substantival representative 'being' are just empty words?

Suppose we try another approach. Suppose we choose 'I am' as a starting point; the Cartesian assertion of my own *being*. But what and where is this *being* of mine? And what about other verbal forms; what about 'was', 'were', 'have been'? Clearly we can hardly hope to be able to derive a clear and unequivocal meaning of *being* from an analysis of particular inflected forms of 'to be'. An analysis of these forms seems to show in fact that this is not possible at all.

D*

It only reveals the vagueness of 'to be'. Is then the word 'being' —to echo a question of Heidegger's—merely another name for this vagueness?

The difficulty of finding a uniform and unequivocal meaning of 'to be' explains why many philosophers deny that 'being' (as the substantival counterpart of the verb) has any discernible philosophical significance on its own. They argue that 'to be' is syncategorematic in the sense of being an incomplete expression incapable of independent meaning. This, they maintain, applies even more to its inflected forms and derivatives which receive what meaning they have exclusively from the context in which they are used.

Heidegger does not accept this view. 'To be' and 'being' may be vague, yet they are not so vague as to be unintelligible out of sentential context. They are not wholly indeterminate. We understand, says Heidegger, the general difference between 'to be' and 'not-to-be'. We understand what it means that something exists—say, this book on the table—not merely because we are able to perceive it but because we are able to understand the possibility of its not being there and indeed not existing at all. In any case—Heidegger points out—the *being* of a thing (his special interpretation of the word 'existence' prevents us here from saying 'the existence of a thing' although this is what the expression 'the being of a thing' means in simple terms) must not be confused with this thing itself. The being of *A* is not the same as *A*; nor can the being of *A* be explained in terms of the conditions under which *A* can be identified, for it is not so much the conditions themselves as our understanding of what these conditions mean that matters here, and this understanding, according to Heidegger, already presupposes a rudimentary understanding of the meaning of 'being'.

The meaning of 'being' and the world of existents

However, the problem is to explain what it is exactly that we do understand. 'Being', according to Heidegger, does not refer to anything that can be found among things. 'Being' is not a name of an existent or a class of existents. But what exactly does it mean? Are we not perhaps deluding ourselves after all in thinking that this word carries a special meaning, although we are unable to articulate this meaning? Are we not (to use Heidegger's own word) in danger of falling a victim to a mere word fetish? 'Being' designates nothing that we could point our finger at. It is not a generalisation of the various uses of 'is'. It is not a generic word like 'tree' or 'chair'. If it were, we would be able to illustrate its meaning by pointing at individual members of the class of things it stands for. But it does not designate any class of things. What is it then?

Heidegger agrees that it is not possible here to give any direct definition in the ordinary sense, but he claims that this is due to the fact that 'being' is inexplicable in terms of existents of any sort and not to a lack of understanding of 'being' on our part. Here is an interesting example from his *Introduction to Metaphysics* which might help to explain what he means. 'Over there, across the road'— he writes—'there is a high school building. An existent (*etwas Seiendes*). We can examine the building from outside from all angles, we can go in and explore it from the basement to the attic, and note everything that is to be found inside: corridors, staircases, classrooms, and their furniture and equipment. Everywhere we find existents, and moreover we find them in a very definite arrangement. Now where is the being of this high school? For after all the school *is* (it exists). The building *is*. If anything belongs to this existent, it is its being; yet we do not find this being inside it. Nor does the being of a thing consist in the fact that we observe it. The building stands there even if we do not observe it. We can find it only because it already *is*. Besides, this building's being does not by any means seem to be the same for everyone. For us, who just look at it or ride by, it is different from what it is for the pupils who sit inside it; not because they see it only from within, but because they actually look at this building under the aspect of what it is and the way it is. One can, as it were, smell the being of this building, and often, many years later one can still feel this same smell in one's nostrils. This smell communicates the being of this existent far more directly and veritably than any description or inspection could ever do. Yet the being of this building cannot be said to be based on this odorous substance floating somewhere in the air.'[1]

'Being', then, does not designate a thing or a property of a thing. It represents—according to Heidegger—something entirely different and unique; something that cannot be objectified and hypostatised in any way. Heidegger criticises traditional metaphysics for ignoring this fact and for confusing 'being' with 'substance'. Traditional metaphysics, says Heidegger, lived in the 'obliviousness of being'. Instead of inquiring into the *being qua being*, it inquired into the *existent qua existent*. It talked of substance, of transcendent entities, of things, of the manifestations of *being* in different ontological regions, never being able to grasp the real meaning of the fundamental ontological difference between *being* and *existents*, and, consequently, never being able to see the problem of *being* in the right perspective.

In more recent times some phenomenological logicians have committed the same metaphysical error by regarding both *being*

[1] ibid., p. 25 ff.

and *non-being* as *objects*. The roots of this error can be traced to the correspondence theory of truth. According to the correspondence theory, truth represents an agreement of thought (expressed in a judgement) with the facts. Consequently, if I judge correctly, e.g. that *A* exists, or that *B* does not exist, the theory seems to require that there should be a fact in each case for my judgements to correspond to. These 'facts'—the being of *A* and the non-being of *B*—will be the objects of my judgements. The oddity of such objects was not regarded as a sufficient reason for discarding the theory. It was argued that the object of a judgement can be anything that can be an object of thought.

Brentano already attacked this view. According to Brentano, *being* and *non-being* belong to the class of *entia irrealia*, fictional entities, which cannot function as genuine objects of thought, let alone exist as objects *per se*. If we adopted the view that *being* is an object, says Brentano, we would soon find ourselves involved in an infinite regress. For by asserting the being of *A* we would, by implication, be also asserting the being of the being of *A*, and so on *ad infinitum*. But to assert the being of *A* does not mean asserting the existence of an object distinct from *A*; it means simply saying that *A* exists. As in the case of all other *irrealia*, so here too—according to Brentano—we are misled by a spurious referring expression ('the being of . . .') into assuming the existence of a completely imaginary entity.

Heidegger would agree entirely with Brentano's criticism of the view that the being of a thing may be regarded as an object, but he would reject decidedly the suggestion that 'being' is no more than a linguistic fiction. Brentano was right, he would say, in thinking that 'the being of . . .' refers to no object, but this fact does not deprive 'being' of meaning and Brentano failed to explain what this meaning is. No linguistic conjuring trick will help us to dispose of this problem. We may try to eliminate certain dubious referring expressions and translate statements in which such expressions occur into straightforward existential propositions, but, according to Heidegger, this will still leave us with the problem of explaining the origins of our intuitive understanding of *being* revealed in such propositions.

'Being, 'non-being' and *Dasein*

But the question again arises how do we make clear what it is that we do understand in the first place, and it soon becomes obvious that, in reply to this question, Heidegger can do no more than to repeat his old statement that we understand *being* because we understand *non-being* (*Nichtsein*). Our understanding of 'something being there', from Heidegger's standpoint, must be seen as ultimately rooted in our understanding of the possibility of 'something not being there'. Or, to use that handy word 'existence', ignoring for the moment the special meaning which Heidegger gives to it: we can understand what the existence of a thing or a state of affairs means because we can understand what the possibility of their *non*-existence means.

According to Heidegger, *being* and *non-being* are interrelated and neither of them can in any way be explained in terms of existents or relations between existents. But let us pause for a moment and ask what *non-being* really means. Does the simple fact that we are able to understand the possibility of 'something not being there' entitle us to look beyond 'not' to an ontological *non-being*? Why, we may ask, should a simple act of negation be assumed to have such metaphysical roots? Is it not possible to explain the origin of 'not' from the differences that we experience among things: from the qualitative, quantitative, positional differences which represent the basis of individuation in the world in which we live? After all, when describing a particular thing we are at the same time indicating in what way it differs from—i.e. 'is not'—other things. The 'not' would seem to be ultimately rooted in this difference. When I say that the chair I am looking for is 'not' in this room, this can, it seems, in the final analysis, only mean that all the things that I have found in this room are different from the object I expected to find. But if 'is not' can be explained in terms of 'is different from' what gives us the right to attach to it any special ontological meaning? Why should 'not' be rooted in some obscure ontological *non-being*?

Yet this is precisely what Heidegger implies. From his standpoint, we understand the meaning of 'is' and 'is not' *because* we understand the meaning of *being* and *non-being* generally. But the trouble is that it is difficult to make clear what precisely this understanding consists in. Heidegger simply assumes that we have this understanding and goes on to ask how is this understanding possible. To him, the question about the meaning of *being* is a question about the roots of our *understanding* of being.

It is we ourselves, Heidegger says, who ask the question about the meaning of being; we ask 'what is "being"?' and by this we already reveal an understanding of 'is', although we are not able to define this understanding in precise terms. Consequently, to analyse the question about *being*, according to Heidegger, means in the first place clarifying the being of a particular existent—the *questioner*. In short, in order to be able to answer the question about the meaning of being we must analyse the being of *Man*.

Man, according to Heidegger, is the existent which holds the

key to both *being* and *non-being* and in order to explain these it is
necessary to analyse Man's own manner-of-being. This is why
Heidegger begins his philosophical analysis of the meaning of being
with an existential analysis of *Dasein*—*Dasein* being his ontological
term for Man. *Dasein*, says Heidegger, is the existent which lives in
the 'understanding of being'; it is the place where being 'discloses
itself'; it is literally the 'there' of *being*. (*Dasein* has in fact been
translated by 'being-there', but this is such an ugly and misleading
construction that it is better avoided.) *Dasein*, then, is the object
of Heidegger's analysis. The definition he gave of *Dasein* has since
become the standard definition of existentialist ontology. According
to this definition, *Dasein* is an existent for which, in its being, this
very being is in question. A stone is indifferent to its being. *Dasein*,
on the other hand, relates himself to his own being, and this being
to which he relates himself is his existence.

The 'essence' of *Dasein* (and therefore of Man), Heidegger says,
is in its *existence*. He writes the word 'essence' in inverted commas,
indicating that the word is used only in its metaphorical sense and
refers to no object or substance in the traditional sense. *Dasein*'s
existence is not an existent, an object. It is not a *what*, but a *how*.
Existence, to Heidegger, is an ontologico-*modal* category. The
interpretation which Heidegger gives to the word 'existence' certainly
differs from the meaning that is usually attached to it, although he
claims that his interpretation is much closer to the etymological
meaning of the word. To him 'existence' means 'ek-sistence', the
prefix 'ek' (out) indicating the *Dasein*'s (i.e. Man's) characteristic
way of existing. *Ek-sistence*—he explains in his peculiar prose—is
the 'ecstatic living in the proximity of being. It is watchkeeping,
i.e. concern about being'.[1] Man *ek*-sists and this means that he is
able to 'stand outside of himself', to withdraw from the immediate
reality of the world that surrounds him. He is a being-in-the-world
and, at the same time, someone who can look at himself and at the
world 'from a distance'. He *ek*-sists and it is because he *ek*-sists
that he can understand the meaning of *being* and *non-being*, of *to be*
and *not-to-be*, of *is* and *is not*.

But did we not encounter similar thoughts in Scheler's anthropology? Heidegger, we said earlier, is not an anthropologist; yet
it cannot be denied that his analysis ultimately rests on the same
presuppositions as that of Scheler. Scheler too looks at Man as
someone who *ek*-sists, who can 'stand outside of himself' and who
is for this very reason able to discover the contingency of everything
existent. It is precisely as someone who *ek*-sists that Man is able
to understand the possibility of non-being and that he begins to

[1] See 'Brief über den Humanismus', in *Wegmarken* (Frankfurt a.M. 1967), p. 173.

wonder 'why there are things rather than nothing'. Both for Scheler and Heidegger this question, which they both consider to be the most crucial and most fundamental of questions, marks the beginning of metaphysics. Quite irrespective of the differences between their metaphysical systems, the fact remains that they both, in the final analysis, build on the same foundations.

II

FROM MODAL ANALYSIS TO
MYSTICAL HERMENEUTICS

Heidegger claims that in his *Sein und Zeit* the question about the meaning of *being* was raised and developed expressly as a question for the first time in the history of philosophy.[1] He claims to have broken entirely new ground by the manner in which he analysed this question, and, in consequence of this, to have given ontology a new significance. He calls his ontology 'fundamental' because in it he is concerned with what he regards as the basic presuppositions of every ontological, and indeed metaphysical reflection. He asks 'What is *being*'? or, expressed more clearly perhaps, 'Where does "to be" derive its meaning?' and this leads him to the 'existential analysis of *Dasein*' as the fundamental ontological analysis.

We said that a crucial difference between his standpoint and that of 'traditional ontology'—as he sees it—consists in the strict distinction he makes between *being* and *existents*. According to him, all idealistic and materialistic ontologies tend to overlook or ignore this distinction. Modern empiricism too makes the same mistake. All these philosophies tend to concentrate their attention on *what* there is (i.e. on existents) instead of on *how* it is (i.e. on *being*). The *how* aspect, the modal aspect, is either neglected or not pursued vigorously to its roots. Or else an attempt is made to explain the *how* from, or reduce it to, the *what*. This among other things is why most philosophers do not realise the fundamental importance of an existential analysis of *Dasein*. They do not see—maintains Heidegger —that only an existential modal analysis can provide us with the key to the meaning of *being*.

[1] See *Einführung in die Metaphysik*, p. 64.

His *Sein und Zeit* purports to give just such an analysis. However, since the publication of *Sein und Zeit* (1927) Heidegger has been trying steadily to present his modal analysis in a wider metaphysical context. In *Sein und Zeit* the subject of analysis was the being of *Dasein*, i.e. *Dasein*'s own manner-of-being. The subsequent development of Heidegger's thought is characterised by the increasing emphasis that he places on *being as such* (as distinct from 'the being of . . .', 'the manner-of-being *of* . . .'). In *Sein und Zeit* the modal analysis of *being* led eventually to the establishing of 'temporality' (*Zeitlichkeit*) as the fundamental ontological modus of *Dasein*; the problem of *being* was approached from the horizon of *time*. *Dasein*'s (=Man's) own manner-of-being provided the basis for an analysis of the meaning of 'to be' and 'not-to-be', their difference and interdependence. In Heidegger's new phase *being* becomes a kind of metaphysical agent which 'discloses itself' in time; it 'reveals itself' to Man in time. It arranges so to speak for its own truth to be listened to 'in time', without however 'revealing' itself completely. *Being* becomes a mysterious metaphysical force, a kind of *deus absconditus*, a concealed God, who gives an indication of his own presence through *Dasein* in time and speaks at his clearest in the language of poetry. Heidegger's development after *Sein und Zeit* shows him becoming increasingly steeped in mysticism.

Here it is not possible to discuss his philosophical development in any great detail. Nor do I think that, philosophically, much profit would be gained from a closer study of the metaphysico-poetic analysis which features prominently in his new phase. I shall therefore concentrate in this exposition on some focal points of his modal analysis of *Dasein*, limiting myself to pointing only briefly to the direction which his thought has subsequently taken.

Dasein *and the possibility of being*
'what one (essentially) is'

Dasein, according to Heidegger, is an existent which is always 'I myself'. Its being is in each particular case 'my own being'. In other words, the 'essence' of *Dasein* cannot be determined by external observation but only by self-analysis. This is a vital first assumption on which everything else depends.

I (as *Dasein*) relate myself to my own being, but this being of mine is not a substance, a substratum, an object within myself. The self-analysis of *Dasein* does not lead to a 'discovery' of a substantival *ego* in the Cartesian sense. My *being* is not substantival. Heidegger, no less than Husserl—although for different reasons—criticises Descartes for maintaining that the essence of the *ego* consists in a 'thinking substance', a '*res cogitans*'. Descartes,

maintains Heidegger, never really freed himself from the influence
of traditional ontology. His so-called 'new beginning' did not
represent a radical change of attitude—at least as far as the problem
of *being* was concerned. While concentrating his attention on
cogito, says Heidegger, Descartes failed to investigate the meaning
of *sum*. He used *cogito* as a stepping stone to *res cogitans* and found
himself confronted with the old difficulties surrounding the metaphysical concept of substance. His analysis remained in many
respects dependent on medieval ontology and his *res cogitans* shows
conspicuous similarities to the medieval '*ens creatum*'. Which all
goes to show, according to Heidegger, that Descartes was not yet
ready for a radically new approach to the problem of *being*.

The radical change, according to Heidegger, came only with his
own existential analysis of *Dasein*. According to Heidegger, instead
of trying to determine the 'what' of this *Dasein* as an object in a
world of objects, we should try to explain its essence from its existence. And 'existence', as we already know, does not mean to Heidegger the existence of *Dasein* as just another existent, but describes
the essential modal aspect of its being. Man as *Dasein* enjoys a
special position because he *ek*-sists, which means that his being is
'disclosed to him'.

Other existents do not exist in this way. They do not relate
themselves to their own being. They do not ask themselves why
they are here and what their being is. Of course, Man too does not
always ask himself these questions. He too can be indifferent. He
may refuse to concern himself with the problems of his being. But
the difference—Heidegger points out—is in this 'can' and this 'may'.
Man can be indifferent but need not be. For a thing there is no
'can'. A thing is what it is. Man, on the other hand, is capable of
'transcending himself', of seeing what he can become and what he cannot be. It is in this awareness of his own possibilities that Man asserts
himself as existence and, at the same time, finds his own 'essence'.

Dasein, says Heidegger, is 'its own possibility' and because it is
its own possibility it can 'choose' itself, it can 'realise' itself and
it can also 'lose' itself.[1] It is an existent whose whole existential
situation is characterised by *possibility*. In this Heidegger upholds
the view expressed most poignantly by *Sören Kierkegaard*, one of
his predecessors, whose existential dialectic revolved around the
concept of possibility. The concept of possibility has significantly
remained one of the main themes of modern existentialism and is
a chief source of the paradoxes with which this philosophy abounds.

But back to Heidegger: his view of *Dasein* as 'its own possibility'
seems to necessitate a distinction between a mode in which *Dasein*

[1] See *Sein und Zeit* (6th ed., Tübingen, 1949), p. 42.

is what it ought to be and a mode in which it is not what it ought to be. Heidegger uses the terms 'authentic' and 'inauthentic' (*eigentlich, uneigentlich*) to refer to the respective modes of *Dasein*. *Dasein* exists authentically when it is fully aware of its own situation and its own possibilities. Only then does it show what it really is. Of course here too Heidegger insists on the ontological nature of his distinction. He would not accept our characterisation of the two modes in terms of 'ought' and 'ought not' as basic. He is describing what he believes to be an ontological fact, not exhorting anyone to take this or that attitude. But there is no doubt that by describing *Dasein* in the 'mode of authenticity' and by drawing a strict distinction between this mode and the inauthentic states in which *Dasein* 'loses itself', 'flees from itself', etc., he is by implication telling us which way we ought to choose.

This inevitably raises the problem of *freedom*. To Heidegger freedom too is primarily an ontological phenomenon. Freedom is closely connected with possibility, and possibility, as we just saw, is an essential ontological characteristic of *Dasein*. The *Dasein* can 'choose itself' or 'not choose itself', and that it is able to do this is an essential part of its ontological make-up. The actual freedom of choice that we exercise in our everyday life, Heidegger maintains, is rooted in the structural situation of *Dasein* which is characterised by *possibility*.

Directly connected with possibility and freedom is another important category, that of the *future*. *Dasein*, in Heidegger's interpretation, is an existent which can 'stand outside of itself' and project itself towards its own possibilities. By projecting itself towards its own possibilities it lives in the 'dimension of the future'. *Dasein*, says Heidegger, is an existent which is essentially 'ahead of itself'; it is oriented towards the future. But, Heidegger points out, this must not be taken to mean that *Dasein* projects itself towards something which it may or may not become; the phrase 'ahead of itself' is not meant in this sense. *Dasein* cannot become other than what it is. In its self-understanding it projects itself towards what it essentially is, and the ontological mode of this projection is 'ahead of itself'.

At this point, Heidegger's existential dialectic becomes somewhat complicated and in order to understand what he is trying to say we shall have to look a little closer at the ontic and phenomenal foundations of his phenomenologico-ontological analysis. For, like other phenomenologists, he claims to begin with what is immediately accessible and to base his analysis on concrete situations in which we actually find ourselves. His declared aim is to clarify the ontological meaning of these situations.

The various activities of Dasein *as forms of 'care'*

According to Heidegger, *Dasein*'s own experiences, the concrete situations in which *Dasein* finds itself in the course of its life, reveal one general characteristic of its mode of being, its *being-in-the-world*. *Being-in-the-world* is Man's being in his own natural 'habitat'. Man lives 'in a world'. His whole existence is bound up with the existence of a world in which he encounters things and other people. The 'world' is the field of Man's activity. This activity can take a variety of forms; it may be concerned with 'other people' or it may be concerned with things or it may be concerned with ourselves. Take our relationship with other people. We are in a continuous direct or indirect contact with other people, we live with them, work with them, care for them, argue with them, love them, fear them. Similarly, we are in a continuous relationship with things. We observe things, we study them, we make tools and use them, we produce goods, we change our environment. We are in some way or other continuously concerned with things. Last but not least, we are concerned with and about ourselves. All this activity which can take many different forms is referred to by Heidegger under the unifying title of *care* (*Sorge*). The word 'care' is taken here in a much wider meaning and must not be confused with what we ordinarily understand by it. In the context of Heidegger's philosophy it designates a fundamental structural characteristic of *Dasein*.

But we must clarify Heidegger's concept of the world a little further. We said that Man cannot exist without a world. But the world in which he exists is inevitably 'his own world'. Things that we encounter in our experience are not entirely 'neutral' objects in an entirely 'neutral' world. They are *our* objects. They appear as they do as objects for us. As objects of human *praxis* they acquire the character of what Heidegger calls 'handiness' (*Zuhandenheit*). This is especially obvious in the case of tools. But, according to Heidegger, we cannot speak meaningfully at all about a world of objects except in the context of human existence. This does not mean that he is advocating a kind of subjectivism. He only wishes to point out the structural interdependence of Man's existence and Man's world.

None the less this clearly shows how radically different his conception of the world is from the conception which is usually associated with science, according to which the 'world' represents no more than a universe of interconnected things. The world, according to Heidegger, is the sphere of Man's activity and something that is structurally related to Man's own being. This does not mean that things do not exist when not observed, used or thought about by a human being; but it does mean that we cannot meaningfully speak about a 'world' without any reference to Man.

Man's being-in-the-world, as we saw earlier, is, according to Heidegger, his being in a *milieu* in which he encounters things, other people and himself. In this *milieu*—his own 'habitat'—Man is capable of understanding himself and also of *mis*understanding himself. In fact his conception of himself in this *milieu* is often confused and distorted. Man tends to 'lose' himself in the various activities of care. He tends literally to 'forget' himself while going about his daily business, working with 'others', serving 'others', giving himself to them. He takes part in public affairs, engages in political activity, identifies himself with various causes, does things as 'others' do them; he leads, so to speak, the life of 'other people'. He leads in fact an alienated, *self*-estranged life. This mode of being Heidegger designates by the nominalised impersonal pronoun *das Man*, which, depending upon the context, can be variously translated as 'one', 'they', 'people', 'it'. These words are among the most frequently heard in everyday language. 'One does' this or that, because others do this or that; 'it is not done', because others don't do it; 'one is frightened', as anyone would be; 'one wonders', 'one knows', 'one behaves', as people wonder, know, behave, etc. One is everyone and no one. The world of *das Man* is a world in which one lives and does things as 'people' live and do things. In this world Man becomes submerged in a nondescript mediocrity in which he loses his real self.

But does this mean that we cease to be mediocre only when we stop behaving as 'other people' do? Heidegger would naturally deny that this is the implication of his view. He would say that he is simply concerned to show that in the mode of *being* which he calls *das Man* the real understanding of *being* is obscured, not to condemn any form of life which on the surface might show the features characteristic of this mode. But disregarding the obvious weakness of such a reply, how can he be sure that in this mode the real meaning of *being* is in fact obscured? How does one reach that degree of self-understanding which gives one the right to look at *das Man*, ontologically, as a form of 'inauthentic', 'unenlightened' existence? Why does Heidegger suppose that this mode does not reveal the true ontological structure of *Dasein*?

The 'disclosing function' of Angst

Heidegger's reply to the above questions would be to point to the existence of an emotion to which he attaches a great ontological significance. This emotion is *Angst*, anguish. According to Heidegger, *Angst* exposes the self-deceptions of our 'public lives' and brings us face to face with ourselves. *Angst* removes all external support from under our feet; it undermines the cosy certainties of our habits and our beliefs; it shocks us into self-consciousness and enables us to see the true nature of our position. It helps us to discover the basic facts about ourselves and the world, and in this respect *Angst* performs a function comparable, within limits, with that of Descartes' doubt or Husserl's *epoché*.

To Heidegger, *Angst* plays a vital role in Man's 'self-understanding'. It makes Man aware of his basic limitations and his basic possibilities, and because of this it makes a full understanding of Man's own ontological structure as *care* possible. *Angst*, says Heidegger, offers the phenomenal basis for the explicit understanding of the totality of *Dasein*'s being.[1] In *Angst* Man is thrown on to himself and made to see the basic realities of his existence.

It is important, Heidegger points out, to distinguish *Angst* from *fear*. Fear is always a fear of something more or less definite, a thing or person, an existent. The object of *Angst*, on the other hand, is indeterminate. It is not any particular thing; it is being-in-the-world as such. *Angst* reveals to Man his being-in-the-world but only by isolating him, by removing him, as it were, from the immediate context of his everyday life. In thus making him aware of his own position it also reveals to him his own and his world's 'contingency', that is, the possibility of his and his world's not existing, their non necessity. It is *Angst* that, according to Heidegger, leads Man to ask the crucial metaphysical question: 'Why are there things rather than nothing?'

All this explains the importance that *Angst* has in Heidegger's phenomenologico-ontological analysis of *Dasein*. To Heidegger, *Angst* not only provides the necessary phenomenal basis for such an analysis, but also justifies such an analysis. *Angst* makes Man aware of his *ek*-sistence; it reveals to him his basic possibilities, and among these possibilities, says Heidegger, there is also the possibility of death, of the end of existence; the possibility of 'being no longer here'. In *Angst*, says Heidegger in his characteristically obscure language, '*Dasein* faces the nothing of the possible impossibility of its own existence'.[2]

It is important to Heidegger that we should distinguish clearly the philosophico-ontological from the biological aspect of death. Biologically, death is simply the end of life; cessation of certain vital biological processes leading to a general disintegration of cells. Ontologically, Heidegger points out, death represents one of those possibilities which together make up the essence of Man. Man, he says, is *essentially* a being-towards-an-end, a being-towards-death.

[1] ibid., p. 182.
[2] ibid., p. 266.

People might not know about death but this does not make them any less mortal. Whether we accept it or not, the fact is that death is a fundamental 'possibility' of Man and without the knowledge of this possibility Man's self-understanding can never be complete. Not knowing about death or playing down the importance of death or interpreting death merely as a biological phenomenon are, according to Heidegger, only different forms of that self-estrangement to which we fall victim in the impersonal 'they-sphere'. They are characteristic of 'inauthentic existence' and can be recognised as such as soon as we turn our attention to ourselves and become fully aware of our true position.

The 'temporality' of Dasein

Heidegger's next step is to consider what he calls the 'temporality' of *Dasein*. *Angst*, as we have just seen, leads, according to him, to the discovery of the possibility of an end of existence, and therefore of death as a basic ontological fact about *Dasein*. This raises inevitably the problems of temporality and time. Death as a fundamental possibility, as something which is inevitable but is 'not yet', is inseparable from the phenomenon of time. This throws new light on the being of *Dasein*. Heidegger, we saw earlier, defined Man's being as *care*. He now maintains that the activities of *care* can be explained from the modus of *temporality* (*Zeitlichkeit*). The central fact about Man is that he exists under the aspect of time, and it is here that all his activities have ultimately their roots. It is from *temporality*, according to Heidegger, that we are able to understand *care* ontologically; temporality is the 'ontological sense of *care*'.

It is important once again to stress the ontological character of his analysis. He is very anxious to prevent a possible misunderstanding on this point. He does not want to be accused of 'psychologism'. He is too much of a Husserlian to make any concessions in this respect. What he wants to do is to give as exact a phenomenological description as possible of what he regards as the permanent modal features of *Dasein*. It would be useless, according to him, to try to explain temporality in terms of what we ordinarily understand by time. So far from being based on the 'everyday' conception of time, temporality—according to Heidegger—represents the basis for an explanation of the latter. It is an *ontological* phenomenon, an expression of the ontological structure of *Dasein*. We saw earlier that, according to Heidegger, one of the essential characteristics of *Dasein* is that it is 'ahead of itself' and consequently that it lives in the 'dimension of future'. It projects itself towards its own possibilities, among which there is also the possibility of its own end. It is able to 'overcome' its own alienation and 'return' to itself, and the possibility of its doing this explains its understanding of the meaning of both the *future* and the *past*. Temporality, Heidegger says, expresses the structural relationship between past, present and future in *Dasein*. It makes, he says, the unity of existence, the facticity of everyday life and alienation (*Verfallen*) possible; and thus provides the basis for an understanding of the structure of *care* in its totality.[1]

This in essentials is Heidegger's view of *Dasein*. He presents his existential analysis as *Dasein*'s own *self-analysis*; as *Dasein*'s inquiry into the modal aspects of its own being. Such an inquiry cannot be conducted from the position of *das Man*, and according to Heidegger it is imperative that we should move away from this position if we want to understand what 'being' means. If anyone should require further proof that this is possible, says Heidegger, he should think of conscience. We pride ourselves on 'having conscience'. We respect 'people with a conscience'. We speak of the 'voice of conscience'. What we say here, says Heidegger, has a deeper meaning. Conscience calls us back to ourselves from the impersonal 'they-sphere'. It makes us remember our responsibilities. In conscience we are reminded of the 'debt' that we have towards ourselves to be what we are.

The aim of Heidegger's phenomenological analysis of *Dasein* was to clarify the meaning of *Sein* (*being*)—something that, in his view, neither Husserl nor Scheler, nor indeed any other philosopher before him had been able to do in any satisfactory way—and if one succeeds in penetrating the heavy armour of numerous specially coined expressions and sibylline phrases in which he has wrapped up his thoughts one can admire the sheer ingenuity and imagination which he displays in his analysis. However, the final result of his efforts is rather disappointing, for the problem to which he has addressed himself, so far from having been solved, continues to puzzle us. All that Heidegger was able to establish, as we saw, were certain modal characteristics of *Dasein*—temporality being the most fundamental of all. But if the result of his analysis was no more than a philosophical restatement of the fact that we are able to understand the meaning of 'is', 'was' and 'will be' because we are finite beings, then he cannot be said to have achieved much. It is also difficult to see what sense there is in talking—from such a position—about 'being as such' as distinct from 'the being of . . .'. As long as he is talking about the being of *Dasein*, i.e. about *Dasein*'s manner-of-being, his analysis is not so difficult to follow. But Heidegger is not prepared to confine himself to a modal analysis of *Dasein*. He is

[1] cf. ibid., p. 328.

impatient to go further. His metaphysical and mystical inclinations make him see in *being* much more than his modal analysis would warrant. As we pointed out in the beginning, in his new phase he has occupied himself mainly with 'being as such'. But it is not at all clear how a transition from a modal analysis of *Dasein* to 'being as such' can be justified phenomenologically and how we can at all make significant assertions about 'being as such' from what he calls the 'horizon of time'.

It is very difficult to understand what this 'being as such' is, especially since it cannot be compared with, or reduced to, any existent. *Being*, maintains Heidegger, is not an existent and it is also *not* nothing. He warns us to be careful not to confuse the 'nothing' that we 'discover' through *Angst* with *being*. This nothing, according to him, is 'rooted in being' but it is not the same as *being*.

But if *being* is *not* nothing, what is it? It is not nothing, and it is not an existent. This would appear to be a contradiction. But Heidegger does not find this embarrassing. Being, he insists, cannot be defined in an ordinary way. It cannot, strictly speaking, be given a definition at all. It is not a whit more a logical entity than it is a physical entity. It is sometimes entirely different. It is, he says, something 'primordial'. It is the *light* which makes it possible for us to see things, to understand the meaning of existence and at the same time to see the possibility of nothing. Its source, however, remains hidden from us.

This is the gist of Heidegger's teaching about *being* and it is clear that at this point he joins the long and familiar mystical tradition in which poetry and poetic insights have always taken precedence over logical reasoning. He carries on this tradition in his analysis of language. According to him, the light of being 'shines' in language. Language, he says, is the 'house of being'. But the language which, in his opinion, provides the authentic access to the 'truth of being' is not the language of science, but the language of *poetry*. Truth is not to be found in the language of formulae. Heidegger here once again shows his intense dislike of science. To him the language of science is an impoverished and formalised language whose philosophical inferiority is unquestionable. Science by its very nature 'conceals' the truth which poetry alone is destined to reveal. In the post-war years Heidegger concentrated increasingly on the analysis of poetry, trying to clarify what he regarded as the metaphysical truths in poems by poets such as Hölderlin, Rilke, Georg Trakl, Stephan George and others. His own style became increasingly 'poetic' and increasingly obscure. But then according to him thinking and poetry are two things that belong closely together.[1]

[1]cf. *Unterwegs zur Sprache* (Neske Verlag, Pfullingen, 1960), p. 237.

I 2

EXISTENTIALISM BASED ON A
PHENOMENOLOGY OF CONSCIOUSNESS

Heidegger does not accept the label of 'existentialism' for his own philosophy. Considering that his interests, especially in the later stages of his philosophical development, are decidedly metaphysical, his attitude in rejecting the label is not difficult to understand. He regards his own existential analysis as an explication of what to him is the metaphysical 'truth of *being*'. Whereas the existentialists, from his point of view, engage in a kind of philosophical psychology, he conducts his own existential analysis from the point of view of *being* as such.

Existentialism and what is sometimes referred to as the 'Existentialist Movement' have been, especially since the Second World War, almost inseparably connected with the name of *Jean-Paul Sartre*. Sartre was profoundly influenced by Heidegger and this influence, as Gabriel Marcel rightly observed, can be felt on every page of Sartre's main (existentialist) work, *Being and Nothingness*. Nevertheless his own 'existential phenomenology' is of a recognisably different brand. There are many features which divide his position from that of Heidegger especially the later Heidegger—although Sartre does not seem always to have been aware of the differences between his and Heidegger's conception of existence. Speaking of the existentialist philosophical position, he said once that the existentialists, especially the 'atheistic existentialists'—among whom, incidentally, he included Heidegger as well as himself—all 'believe that existence precedes essence—or, if you will, that subjectivity should be our point of departure'.[1] Heidegger rejects the

[1] *L'Existentialisme est un Humanisme* (Paris, 1965), p. 17.

first part of this statement. He considers the dispute over whether existence precedes essence a metaphysical dispute in old style and philosophically sterile. Platonist metaphysics asserts the priority of essence. Sartre (in Heidegger's view) merely reversed this position and the result was yet another metaphysical statement, namely that existence comes before essence. But according to Heidegger the question is not which precedes which. It is not the old metaphysical problem of whether individuals come before universals or the other way round that we must settle. What we must do is to clarify the meaning of existence. To Heidegger, as we saw earlier, existence means *ek*-sistence, and *ek*-sistence, he maintains, is not 'before' essence: *it is* Man's essence.

Heidegger, then, views Man as *ek*-sistence and as someone who for this very reason lives, as he puts it, in the 'truth of *being*'. Man has an important metaphysical task to fulfil in the general scheme of things. He is, says Heidegger in his *Letter on Humanism*, 'called upon by *being* itself to take care of its truth'.[1] By overcoming his own alienation and returning to himself, Heidegger maintains, Man discovers time as the horizon of *being* and recognises the importance of his own ontological role as the medium through which *being* 'discloses itself'.

All this is very different from what Sartre has to say about *being*. Sartre contrasts *being*—which to him represents a kind of undifferentiated plenum—with *conscious existence* and defines self as 'lack of being'. We shall see later that he puts the main emphasis on an analysis of consciousness. Heidegger, whilst disclaiming any connexion between his philosophy and religious commitment, does not in principle exclude such commitment. Sartre on the other hand is a professed atheist. Whereas Heidegger is anxious to stress the importance of the ontological difference between *being* and *existents* and refers to *being* in semi-religious terms, Sartre sees no justification for attaching to *being* mystical attributes.

The most conspicuous general feature of Sartre's type of existentialism is a trend towards 'psychologism' and a lack of reverence for any kind of metaphysics. Heidegger is a metaphysician with strong mystical leanings. Sartre is, or at least was before his conversion to marxism, strongly anti-metaphysical. His main interest is freedom, and freedom he maintains cannot be enclosed within a metaphysical system without being 'destroyed'. We are free, says Sartre, and our prime duty is to preserve this freedom, not to ask what 'metaphysical purpose' this freedom serves.

Ontologically, the freedom that Man possesses characterises Man as someone who is able to 'stand outside of himself'. In this Sartre

[1] *Wegmarken* (*Brief über den Humanismus*), p. 172 f.

echoes the views expressed by Scheler and Heidegger. But he differs from these philosophers in that he does not try to offer a metaphysical 'explanation' of this fact. According to Sartre, we are not 'given' freedom in order to be able to realise the presence of an ever-elusive Absolute, or in order to 'serve the truth of being'. We are free because we are free, and this is all there is to it. Instead of looking for deeper metaphysical reasons behind our ability to make free decisions, we should accept freedom as an absurd and inexplicable fact. It is useless to try to anchor our freedom in a mystical Absolute. We have no other function to perform here except to be what we are. We must accept the absurdity of our situation for what it is. Our only salvation, Sartre maintains, is to exercise our freedom by taking such commitments as will leave to our freedom the widest scope for action.

This view is shared by the majority of the non-religious existentialists. They all put great emphasis on freedom and they all insist on the necessity of action as a means of asserting this freedom; at the same time they regard a radical commitment to any political or religious cause as a potential danger to this freedom. This has set limits to their own much publicised social nonconformism and political rebelliousness. Chary of identifying themselves with any political movement, although leaning towards the Left and hating 'bourgeois' society and 'bourgeois' morals, the majority of them took refuge in literature and art. It is through literature and art that they 'rebelled' and hoped to achieve their own salvation.

We saw that Heidegger too took an intense interest in poetry. But his general attitude was and still remains very different. He looks to poetry for clues to the 'mystery of *being*'. The existentialists, on the other hand (I am here of course excluding the religious existentialists), use literature as a weapon, and as a shield to protect themselves from the absurdity of existence. Heidegger uses poetry as a basis for his mystical hermeneutics. The existentialists use literature and art to attack the hypocrisies and self-deceptions of bourgeois society and to keep themselves afloat in what they regard as an absurd world. In this they carry on, in essentials, the familiar traditions of European Romanticism and could with some justification be called the 'new romantics'.

Sartre's conception of consciousness: the 'pre-reflective cogito'

But we must turn now to Sartre and examine his own theoretical position in some detail. Sartre's 'phenomenological ontology' is on the whole more straightforward than that of Heidegger. It is based entirely on a phenomenological analysis of *consciousness*.

Whereas Heidegger (in his *Being and Time*) concentrated on the analysis of *Dasein*'s manner-of-being in an effort to explain the meaning of *being*, Sartre devotes his whole attention to the analysis of consciousness. We cannot, he claims, understand the existential situation of Man without analysing the structure of consciousness. Consequently he takes consciousness as his point of departure.

But what is consciousness? How do we set about analysing consciousness? Every consciousness—says Sartre, echoing the view expressed earlier by Husserl—is a consciousness *of* something. An 'act of consciousness' is an intentional, thetic act. Let it be said at once, however, that Sartre while accepting the intentionalist theory of consciousness is entirely out of sympathy with Husserl's transcendentalism. His views are in fact much closer to those of Brentano than to those of Husserl. Sartre's main concern is to show that mental acts are conscious acts and that the consciousness in these acts represents something that can never be objectified and hypostatised.

The consciousness that I have, say, of experiencing a pleasure or of seeing a chair cannot, Sartre maintains, be dissociated from my experiencing this pleasure or seeing this chair. Consciousness is part of the act and is not 'self-positional' in the sense of positing itself as well as the object. In other words an act in which I am conscious of having something as an object does not imply the existence of consciousness as a *special kind of entity*. Consciousness is not an object; nor can it be turned into one in an act of 'self-consciousness'. The assumption of a consciousness of consciousness as a consciousness of an object would lead to an infinite regress of consciousness of consciousness of consciousness, etc. We saw earlier that Brentano had already exposed the absurdity of this view.

Consequently, the first conclusion that we must draw is that consciousness is *not* substance-like. It cannot be studied as an object can be studied. It is, Sartre says, an 'absolute of existence and not of knowledge'. This, he thinks, should be sufficient to dispose of the Cartesian metaphysics. Consciousness cannot be objectified into a Cartesian *ego*. Consciousness, says Sartre, has in itself 'nothing substantial, it is pure "appearance" in the sense that it exists only to the extent to which it appears'.[1]

But does this mean that what we call 'self-consciousness' is a mere illusion, that there can be no real self-consciousness? Not at all, says Sartre. Every positional consciousness of an object, he says, is at the same time a 'non-positional', 'non-thetic' consciousness of itself. In an act in which I posit an object, I have at the same time a non-thetic self-consciousness of my involvement in this act. For

[1] *L'Etre et le Néant* (Paris, 1950), p. 23.

this no special act of reflection is needed. Every consciousness transcends its object (as consciousness *of* something) and is in some way or other *present* to itself—although it is not necessarily a consciousness of a self. For example, I am perfectly aware of now seeing an orange on the window-sill and could, if asked, report my experience; I am aware of myself having this experience. My consciousness of seeing the orange involves a self-awareness without however being a reflective consciousness of a 'self'. Sartre calls this 'non-thetic' consciousness the 'pre-reflective cogito'.

It is this 'pre-reflective cogito', i.e. the consciousness involved in ordinary mental acts, that he takes as a basis of his phenomenological inquiry. One could describe the subject of his analysis as 'consciousness in action'. This consciousness, whilst 'present to itself', is not self-positing. It is present to itself not as an *entity*, but as what Sartre calls an 'operative intention'. In contrast to the Cartesian 'static' conception of consciousness, Sartre takes a 'dynamic' view of consciousness. The 'static' conception of consciousness, according to Sartre, leads to an attempt to infer existence from knowledge ('I think, therefore I am'). The 'dynamic' view of consciousness, on the other hand, makes it possible for us to look at knowledge as an *existential* phenomenon.

Sartre, then, emphasises the *existential* aspect of consciousness. His main thesis is that the awareness that we have of our doing something, experiencing something, etc., is of a non-reflective kind and does not involve the positing of a self as an object. Existence, maintains Sartre, comes before 'objectifying knowledge'. This, among other reasons, is why he rejects the Cartesian doctrine of substance. Descartes, as we saw earlier, uses *cogito* to infer 'I exist as a thinking substance'. Sartre rejects this inference, as indeed all other phenomenologists do. He rejects the idea of the ego as a 'finished product'. The ego, he maintains, is not a substance which somehow 'inhabits' our consciousness. The self is not a hypostatised essence lurking in the depth of my being. It is an 'ideal', a 'limit', something which I am constantly projecting as a fulfilment of my acts, but which I can never say I 'possess' as an object, it is something which is given to me as a constant 'absent present'. The *self*, in other words, is constantly in the process of *making*.

However, this is one of the more obscure parts of Sartre's doctrine, and before discussing this problem any further we must return once again to the phenomenon of consciousness and analyse the ontological interpretation given to it by Sartre.

The For-itself *and the* In-itself—
two fundamental modes of being

According to Sartre consciousness characterises a mode of being fundamentally distinct from that of the non-conscious or the 'opaque' world of objects. He uses two Hegelian terms to distinguish consciousness from the non-conscious world: *For-itself* and *In-itself*. What he means by the In-itself is best illustrated by an example he gave in his book on *Imagination*. 'I look'—he writes—'at this white sheet of paper lying on my desk. I perceive its shape, its colour, its position. These different qualities have certain things in common. First of all, each presents itself as something which I can merely register as being there, as something whose existence does not in any way depend on my whim. They are there *for* me, but they are not *myself*. Nor are they *somebody else*. In other words, they are not dependent on anyone's spontaneity, either that of my consciousness or that of somebody else's consciousness. They are present and inert at the same time. This inertness of the content of perception, which has often been described, is being-in-itself.'[1]

By contrast, consciousness—according to Sartre—appears 'as a pure spontaneity confronting the world of things which is pure inertness'. The In-itself is non-conscious and opaque. The For-itself is conscious and transparent. Both these types of being, according to Sartre, are revealed through what he calls the 'human reality' —a category which approximately corresponds to Heidegger's *Dasein*.

Once the vital distinction between the In-itself and the For-itself has been drawn, Sartre, not surprisingly, gives especial attention to the analysis of the latter. In this analysis he shows himself to belong, in spite of sundry disagreements, to a tradition which goes back beyond Heidegger to Nietzsche and Kierkegaard. For it is not difficult to recognise in his For-itself yet another version of that suffering 'subjectivity' which plays such an important role in romantic philosophies of various kinds. This subjectivity is the subjectivity of a free and lonely individual for whom the objective world and its categories have lost all real meaning and who hopes to find his own salvation through an exclusive religious relationship with a transcendent 'Absolute', or by accepting the absurdity of his situation and insisting on a 'heroic existence' in face of the absurd. Being an atheist, Sartre chose the latter path. But some years ago his solitary heroism seems to have failed him, for he too began to seek 'ideological protection' and in his *Critique of Dialectical Reason* (*Critique de la Raison Dialectique*, 1960) tried to shelter behind Marx and historical materialism.

[1] *L' Imagination* (Paris, 1963), p. 1.

But we must take a closer look at the For-itself and its basic ontological features. According to Sartre, the key to the ontological structure of the For-itself lies in the phenomenon of *negation*. What does he mean by this? A clue can be found in the example which we quoted earlier. I perceive this white sheet of paper in front of me and I am aware of its existence as something *different* from myself. (Note that here 'different from' comes in very useful for clarifying the meaning of 'not'.) I am different from the object that I perceive, I am *not* it. Seeing an object, in a sense, is an act by which I separate myself from it. I see an object as an In-itself and am at the same time aware that I cannot look at myself in the same way, and that consequently I myself cannot be an In-itself. I am *not* an In-itself. I cannot *objectify* my own consciousness, for in consciousness I *transcend* the world of objects.

This result of psychological introspection receives in Sartre's philosophy a wider ontological interpretation. According to this interpretation, the For-itself comes into being through an act of *negation* of its identity with the In-itself. The For-itself asserts its own difference from the In-itself, and in the very act in which it does this reveals itself, according to Sartre, as a 'lack' and as 'its own nothingness'. Expressed in more simple terms, this means that I, while transcending, in consciousness, the world of objects, find myself face to face with a nothingness within myself, i.e. I find that consciousness is different from anything substantival. What I 'lack', according to Sartre, is a self as an *object*. I realise that I am not an In-itself, and that insofar as I am not an In-itself nothingness forms an essential part of my being.

Like Heidegger Sartre attaches to negation a deep ontological significance. Negation, maintains Sartre, is not merely a 'quality of judgement'; it is not something that belongs exclusively to propositions. It is not merely a logical phenomenon. It is primarily an ontological phenomenon and as such it is closely related to the ontological structure of consciousness. Logical negation, maintains Sartre, presupposes a 'pre-judicative' understanding of *non-being*; we would not be able to form and to understand negative judgements unless we were able to understand the meaning of *non-being*. 'The necessary condition for our saying *not*'—he writes— 'is that *non-being* remains permanently present within us and outside of us, that nothingness *haunts* being.'[1]

For Sartre, the significance of negation consists in the fact that it points to that *nothing* which, in his view, represents an essential part of our ontological make-up and is rooted in the very nature of consciousness. For since consciousness implies a permanent

[1] *L'Etre et le Néant*, p. 47.

transcendence over the In-itself and has in itself nothing 'substantial', it can only be through consciousness, and hence through Man —says Sartre—that *nothing* 'comes to the world'. It is through consciousness that Man puts himself outside *being* and by this, in Sartre's phrase, 'weakens its structure'.

The link between nothingness, freedom and anguish

As we can see, the essentials of Sartre's ontology are very simple, much more so than his obscure language would suggest. Everything hinges ultimately on his view of consciousness as that elusive unobjectifiable something which hovers, as it were, above the inert mass of the In-itself. This consciousness is the essence of the human subjectivity, the For-itself; and it is through this consciousness, this no-thing, this *nothing* which we carry within ourselves that we are able to 'disengage ourselves from *being*' and look at things, as it were, from a distance.

According to Sartre our ability to transcend what he calls the 'sheer positivity' of *being* is illustrated in the most remarkable way by our ability to ask questions. Every question, Sartre says, posits already the possibility of a negative reply. Asking a question pre-supposes the possibility of a 'nihilating withdrawal', the ability of looking beyond what there is towards what there is not or what there might be. In the question, we 'detach' ourselves from *being* and posit the possibility of both *being* and *non-being*. All this, Sartre maintains, has a wider significance, for our ability to 'disengage ourselves from *being*' (which is illustrated by our ability to ask questions) represents at the same time the basis of our *freedom*.

This brings us at once to what is undoubtedly the most familiar and the most popular aspect of existentialist philosophy. The theme of freedom has always been one of the great philosophical themes but existentialism has in a special way made this theme its own. In his phenomenological analysis of consciousness Sartre tries to explain what he thinks are the ontological foundations of freedom. We are free, he maintains, because we are capable of a 'nihilating withdrawal' and of 'disengaging ourselves from *being*'. These two phrases sum up what in his view represents our basic ontological position. Sartre sees Man as someone who in consciousness transcends the reality of objects, and who because of this can resist external influence, say 'no', exercise choice and make his own decisions. Man's essence is in his freedom and his prime responsibility towards himself is the responsibility of acknowledging and asserting this freedom. But, while doing this, he must be prepared at the same time to face the abyss of nothingness at the very heart of his being. For freedom, in the final analysis, is only an expression

E

of that 'original nihilation' which puts Man beyond the In-itself and which, as a result, denies him a firm hold both externally and internally. Freedom implies 'transcending' both the world of 'external objects' and that of one's own past experiences; it means being free to 'create' one's own future and, at the same time, being obliged to take full responsibility for one's own actions.

This can be burdensome, and not surprisingly we often feel reluctant to face the fact that we are completely free. We are, says Sartre, anguished by our freedom. We are uneasily aware of the gap that exists between our past and our future, between what we are and what we could be, between our acts and our possibilities. Anguish, says Sartre, arises from my knowledge that 'nothing can insure me against myself'. There is no one to whom I could turn for help; I cannot accept anyone's authority except my own; I give meaning to the world; I create values; at the same time, I am unable to explain the origin of my freedom. In anguish, according to Sartre, I am anguished by the fact that my freedom is the foundation of values while itself being *without* a foundation.

According to Sartre, we spend most of our time trying to flee from this anguish and avoid the responsibilities that our freedom imposes on us. We tend to hide 'behind other people's backs' and let others make our decisions for us. We are prepared to live the life of tools rather than accept the burden of responsibility for making our own decisions. This refusal to face the truth about ourselves Sartre calls 'bad faith'. In 'bad faith', according to Sartre, we try to 'fill up' somehow the 'nothingness which we are in relation to ourselves'; we pretend to be something other than what we are; we try to hide from ourselves the fact that we are completely free.

All this is very much reminiscent of what Heidegger said about the impersonal world of *das Man* and Sartre's debt to Heidegger in this as in many other things is considerable. As we saw earlier, Heidegger looks at *das Man* as a form of 'inauthentic existence'. In the impersonal 'they-world' of *das Man* we tend to 'lose ourselves' by trying to live as 'other people' live and behave as 'other people' do; we literally lead a self-estranged life in which the truth about ourselves remains 'hidden from us'. The way back to ourselves and to 'authentic existence' leads away from *das Man*, away from the crowd, or, as Sartre would say, away from the alienation of 'bad faith'.

At this point we must revert briefly to Sartre's conception of the 'self'. We said earlier that, according to Sartre, the self cannot be an object, or else it would fall within the domain of the In-itself. The self is not a kind of ego-substance. But what, then, is self, and how can it be determined? Sartre's answer involves some complicated dialectical reasoning. The self, he says, represents an ideal distance within the immanence of the subject in relation to himself. It is something that is permanently in the process of completion. It is present to itself 'as absent'. In other words, I do not find myself as a special kind of object within myself in addition to my experiences. Sartre here, in effect, endorses the view already held by Hume who said that 'when I enter most intimately into what I call *myself*, I always stumble on some particular perception or other, of heat or cold, light or shade, love or hatred, pain or pleasure'.[1] However, Sartre wants to point out that it is I who am here talking about myself. It is I who am unable to find myself as an entity and this points to a *division* within myself, it points to the fact that I exist as a 'lack of coincidence with myself'. The characteristic feature of the self, according to Sartre, is that it does not 'coincide with itself' in the sense in which an unconscious object may be said to 'coincide with itself'.

Sartre relies here clearly on his analysis of consciousness. The essence of consciousness, according to him, is to exist 'at a distance from itself as a presence to itself'. Consciousness inevitably involves self-consciousness; it involves transcendence, and this is reflected in the structure of the self. The self's activity is directed towards an ideal of 'totalisation' which can never be materialised. The self, according to Sartre, is a never-ending process of *self-completion*.

To conclude, the main result of Sartre's phenomenological analysis of consciousness is that consciousness is not objectifiable, that it cannot be explained away, that it involves a permanent transcendence of the world of objects. Hence what Sartre calls our 'indeterminacy' and our freedom. Hence the 'absurdity' (i.e. absolute inexplicability) of our existence. Hence the nothingness that we harbour within ourselves and the feeling of anguish. Freedom, nothingness, anguish —these are found to be the chief ingredients of that subjectivity which, according to Sartre, existentialism takes as its 'point of departure' and which, we may add, it never really leaves.

Sartre's analysis gives a very sombre picture of Man's existential situation. Certainly one is bound to find oneself in a very unenviable position once one has gathered enough courage to 'return to oneself' from self-estrangement in 'bad faith'. On Sartre's existential diagnosis, my freedom renders me an absolute miracle in the world. It also reveals to me the fact that I am a 'contingent' being. I am made to realise the complete gratuitousness of my own existence. This inevitably increases my feeling of insecurity. Everything I do reveals to me my own limitations. I cannot rely on anyone or

[1] *Treatise*, bk. I, pt. IV, sect. VI.

anything except my own freedom; but this freedom offers me no comfort, for it only reveals to me the absurdity of my existence. It shows me that I might as well not be here, that I am not necessary, that I am absolutely dispensable; it shows me, as Sartre puts it, that I am *de trop*.

Another problem for me is the difficulty of establishing, from the 'standpoint of subjectivity', the right kind of communicative contact with my fellow human beings. Sartre devoted a large part of his *Being and Nothingness* to the problem of 'others', trying to show that his view of existence so far from leading to solipsistic conclusions proves the indispensability of 'others' to the individual. Being-for-itself and what he calls being-for-others are, according to him, two equally essential modes of the 'human reality'. Without 'others' and without my being able to communicate with them I could not develop as an individual; without them, says Sartre, I would not be what I am. And yet, from Sartre's standpoint, these 'others' cannot help me in any way in my predicament. They cannot change my basic situation. My life with them is full of conflict and tension. They seem to be there to remind me of the precariousness of my own situation rather than to help me to get over my difficulties. What advantage then do I have in knowing that I am not alone?

In view of all this it is quite understandable why, for example, Albert Camus should regard suicide as 'the one truly serious philosophical problem'. If life has no purpose, if my freedom makes me so unhappy and so vulnerable, if no religious or social commitment can protect me from the absurdity of existence, why should I go on living and thus unnecessarily prolonging my troubles? This was Camus' dilemma and he decided that to end life would be an admission of defeat. It would be a cowardly act unworthy of Man and his rebellious nature. If we are to assert our human dignity, Camus maintains, we must defy the absurd by accepting life as it is. Well, not quite as it is. As Nietzsche said 'we have art in order not to die of truth'; and Camus, who decided in favour of life, sought salvation in his own art. And Sartre did so too.

13

SARTRE'S ROAD TO MARXISM

Husserl—we saw earlier—in an effort to avoid psychologism whilst at the same time wishing to do justice to the 'subjective' aspect of knowledge, conducted his analysis from the standpoint of 'transcendental subjectivity' and 'transcendental consciousness'. Sartre, on the other hand, conducted his own analysis from the standpoint of 'existential subjectivity' and 'existential consciousness'. It was the existential aspect that Sartre emphasised. Husserl's transcendentalism was too remote from the realities of human existence as well as creating insuperable philosophical difficulties. Husserl's programme of 'phenomenological constitution' was manifestly a failure. It seemed that unless one was prepared to abandon the phenomenological approach for some kind of constructivist metaphysics there was only one option left open: to concentrate on a phenomenological analysis of 'existential subjectivity' and, in particular, to explore the field of emotions. Sartre did just this, but the manner in which he did it showed him to be closer to the romantic thinkers of the past than he may have imagined himself to be, and this inevitably brought him within firing range of two stern critics: *Hegel* and *Marx*.

Hegel's criticism of romanticism is to be found in his *Phenomenology of the Spirit*, especially in the chapter on 'Morality' in which Hegel discusses the subjectivity of 'moral consciousness'. The section on 'Unhappy Consciousness' in the same book is also highly relevant.[1] Hegel mentions no names; he is not concerned with indi-

[1] Although Hegel in this section has in mind certain specifically Christian attitudes, what he has to say provides valuable insights into the 'romantic mentality'.

vidual philosophers but with philosophical *attitudes* (although while writing he often has concrete people in mind); he is analysing the forms of consciousness, in this case the forms of subjective consciousness, and trying to expose the contradictions they engender—the contradictions which, in his view, lead inevitably to higher forms of experience and a more complete self-knowledge on the part of the Spirit. From Hegel's point of view, the romantic subjective consciousness is characterised by its 'negativity', by its inability to 'externalise' itself and to understand the objective, the *inter-subjective*, world. One of Hegel's main aims was precisely to rehabilitate philosophically that 'objective reality' which, he thought, was lost to the subjective consciousness. Marx in a different way tried to achieve the same goal. He too tried to rehabilitate the 'objective reality', although his own interpretation of this reality was very different from that of Hegel's. What both he and Hegel were agreed upon was that the 'standpoint of subjectivity' was negative and sterile and that it was necessary to go beyond it, to 'transcend' it, if one wanted to obtain a more balanced as well as a more accurate picture of the world. Sartre now himself feels the inadequacy of the 'standpoint of subjectivity', and in his current efforts to strike a dialectical balance between subjectivity and objectivity he takes *Marx* as his guide.

Sartre revised his earlier position and, significantly, this revision involved the acceptance by him of certain assumptions which could no longer be explained or justified on a purely phenomenological basis. We saw that Heidegger, for his part, tried to incorporate his own existential phenomenological analysis of *Dasein* into a wider metaphysical framework and made assertions about *being* which could not be justified in purely phenomenological terms. The difference between him and Sartre, however, is that while he (Heidegger) was led by his preoccupations with *being* towards mysticism, Sartre moved from the position of his existential phenomenology to marxism.

Romanticism, Hegel and Marx

But before explaining Sartre's new position it is necessary to say a little more about romanticism, Hegel and Marx. A brief historical retrospect will help to clarify the background against which both Sartre's earlier views and his conversion to marxism can better be understood.

European romanticism began its life as a movement of rebellious intellectuals in a situation of wide-spread political and social unrest. The disintegration of the old feudal social structure and the advent of the new bourgeois society which was politically inaugurated by the French Revolution of 1789, created a situation which favoured the growth of romantic philosophies. The idea of freedom was the dominant idea of the age. Freedom was the main theme in politics, freedom was the main theme in the arts, and freedom was the main theme in philosophy. The *Revolution*, being itself a political manifestation of the intellectual emancipation from tradition achieved in the Age of Enlightenment, furthered the cause of emancipation in all spheres of social life. Throughout Europe, with the exception of Russia, the old feudal world was on the wane. The old values were collapsing and new values had to be found to replace them. This caused a great deal of excitement, but it also created a considerable moral confusion. The increasing fragmentation of the once closely knit social texture brought feelings of uneasiness and insecurity. It was clear that many of the old political and social institutions could not last and would eventually disappear totally, but it was not clear what ought to come in their place. The parvenu society of the bourgeois class was based on the principle of ruthless competition and offered no protection to the individual. Greater freedom brought greater insecurity. As a result the general political and intellectual malaise was intensified. Characteristically the loss of contact with tradition induced an obsessive interest in the past. It was during this period that many national myths were created. Nationalism as we know it today is in many ways a romantic invention. It was the romantics who popularised the idea of 'national heritage'; they discovered folklore; they led the movements for 'national reawakening'; they were in the forefront of all battles for 'national liberation'. Nationalism filled the vacuum created by the disintegration of the old social order and offered, in a sense, an emotional protection against the cold realities of the new bourgeois freedom. But it soon became obvious that nationalism could not solve any of the problems troubling the free and lonely romantic individual. In fact, a great many romantic intellectuals who greeted the French Revolution and its message of freedom with enthusiasm found themselves in the subsequent years psychologically homeless. Some of them (like Hegel, for example) sought a way out of the intellectual confusion bequeathed by the *Revolution* by constructing elaborate all-embracing metaphysical systems which were nothing but forms of secularised religion. But many found the 'philosophical absolutism' of idealistic metaphysics just as abhorrent as the political absolutism, accusing both of trying, each in its own way, to crush the individual and his freedom. Restless and rebellious by nature, these latter intellectuals persisted in their individualism, often seeking to relieve their situation through an extravagant religiosity or a passionate interest in the arts. It is primarily to these intellectuals that we refer here as 'romantics'.

It is against the attitudes of these intellectuals that Hegel's criticism is directed. To Hegel, the romantics' insistence on subjective freedom is merely a sign of intellectual immaturity. The romantic consciousness, to him, is an immature, philosophically underdeveloped consciousness whose troubles and difficulties must be regarded as signs of the growing pains of Reason. The romantic consciousness is lonely and homeless because it has not found the right bearings and is unable to find its way about in the objective world. It drifts aimlessly, vainly trying to compensate for its loneliness and for the disharmony that it feels within itself by trying to achieve a 'happy synthesis' within its own subjectivity. But this subjective synthesis, according to Hegel, is chimerical and cannot help the romantic subjective consciousness out of its predicament. So long as it persists in the attitude of 'subjectivity' this consciousness will never be able to come to terms with reality and genuinely relieve its unhappiness.

The stand that Sartre took during his 'existentialist period' is highly reminiscent of these earlier romantic attitudes. The only difference is that Sartre stated his own views in a much more defiant manner, with no delusions about a 'happy synthesis'. The *human reality*—wrote Sartre—'is by nature an unhappy consciousness with no possibility of overcoming its unhappy state'.[1] Its 'unhappiness' is due to its peculiar ontological position. Sartre, as we saw, defined self as a 'lack'. Indeed the For-itself as a whole is characterised in his ontology as a 'lack'. What the For-itself lacks, according to Sartre, is a certain 'coincidence with itself'. This coincidence can never be achieved if the For-itself is not to cease to be what it is and become something else. The For-itself projects itself constantly towards its self-completion, but this process of 'totalisation' is destined to remain unfinished. The gap within the For-itself, that is, within consciousness, can never be bridged. The For-itself can never become an *object*. According to Sartre, it is here that freedom, anguish and all the problems that torment the *human reality* have their roots.

It is this presumed 'unobjectifiability' of the For-itself that led Sartre to dispute the primacy of what he called 'objectifying knowledge' and to insist on the primacy of existence. We should analyse the knower before analysing the structure of knowledge, he maintained. Existence comes before theory. It is to the knower's existence that we should first turn our attention. This existence cannot be conceptualised and studied in the way objects are studied in science. Its nature can be explored adequately only through *self-analysis* by phenomenological introspection.

But let us return to Hegel. Hegel maintained, in effect, that the

[1] *L'Etre et le Néant,* p. 154.

difficulties of the romantics were due to their stubborn insistence on the 'standpoint of subjectivity', and he was undoubtedly right. But the philosophical solution which he himself proposed had its own unattractive implications. According to Hegel, the subjective consciousness can overcome its difficulties in one way only: by giving up its subjectivistic stance and by recognising the dialectical unity of the 'being-for-itself' and the 'being-in-itself' in what he regarded as the cosmic process of the 'self-unfolding of Absolute Spirit'. The romantics, in other words, should abandon their insistence on the primacy of human subjectivity and accept the fact that this subjectivity represents only one aspect of the 'whole'. Hegel believed he had demonstrated in his own philosophy the dialectical unity of subjectivity and objectivity in 'Absolute Spirit'. His attitude implied that his own philosophy as a final metaphysical synthesis had brought the previously mentioned cosmic process to a close. The 'metaphysical history' of mankind seemed thus to have ended with Hegel. But since this, according to Hegel's critics, constituted a philosophical seal of approval to the continued existence of the Prussian police state, as well as implying that Hegel's philosophy was the ultimate truth, it was a far from comforting prospect to contemplate. If Hegel thought that he had dealt successfully with the 'romantic rebellion' subsequent developments soon proved him wrong. The 'rebels' considered themselves far from beaten.

One of the romantic rebels from the younger generation and one of Hegel's bitterest opponents was *Sören Kierkegaard*. To Kierkegaard, Hegel's metaphysics was a preposterous academic construction which had nothing to do with the real problems of human existence. Hegel had lost himself in his own abstractions. He was like a man who is busily constructing abstruse theories behind the closed doors of his study, hoping that somehow all problems will be solved once they are neatly ordered into a system. What Hegel failed to realise, according to Kierkegaard, was that human subjectivity cannot be incorporated into any such abstract system; this subjectivity cannot be 'objectified': it has got to be *lived*. Existence, maintained Kierkegaard, anticipating Sartre and other existentialists, comes before objectifying knowledge. Kierkegaard's main criticism of Hegel was that he (Hegel) ignored the *existential presuppositions* of his metaphysical constructions. Hegel talked of the 'self-knowledge of Absolute Spirit' instead of concentrating his attention on the existential situation of the *human knower*.

Another great rebel and critic of Hegel was *Karl Marx*. Marx too attacked Hegel's system as an academic attempt to force the dynamic reality of the human world into a preordained metaphysical pattern.

Marx and Kierkegaard underlined the role of Man as a historical agent in his own right. They both were trying to restore to Man his 'natural rights' which they thought were denied to him in Hegel's system of 'Absolute Spirit'. But while they both put the emphasis on Man and his actions as a historical being, they viewed Man, the history-maker, from very different angles. Whereas Kierkegaard emphasised the existential freedom of the individual, Marx insisted that Man should be viewed primarily as a *producer* in a social context. According to Marx, Man 'makes' himself and his own history in the field of production. It is only by studying his activity in the field of production that we can understand his *ideas*. Life—we are told in *German Ideology* (which Marx wrote in collaboration with Engels)—is not determined by consciousness, but consciousness by life. If we are to be able to comprehend the various 'forms of consciousness' we must analyse the mode of production of material life. This was Marx's main thesis and the main point he made in his criticism of Hegel. Whereas Kierkegaard looked at Man as a free and lonely individual whose basic existential situation, he thought, was determined by the relationship this individual has with an ever-elusive Absolute, Marx looked at Man as a social being living and working in a social context, being influenced and formed by this context. Kierkegaard, in his opposition to Hegel, carried on the tradition of romantic individualism. Marx was not an individualist, nor was he interested in religion, except as a social and a historical phenomenon. Marx's anti-hegelianism consisted chiefly in his rejection of Hegel's 'Absolute Spirit' as the 'author' of human history and in the materialist interpretation he gave to the hegelian dialectic. From Marx's point of view, Man makes his own history—Man, that is, as a social being and as a *producer*, not as a 'romantic existence'. Man makes his own history and, at the same time, he is *made by it*.

These are the main ideas underlying Marx's theory of history, his 'historical materialism'. The deep gulf that divides his position from that of Kierkegaard is due simply to the fact that Marx looks at Man and his freedom in an *evolutionary* historical context and makes room for the view of Man as an *object* (of so-called 'historical forces'), thus rejecting by implication the existentialist doctrine of the 'unobjectifiability' of human subjectivity. This is important to bear in mind if we are to understand what is involved in Sartre's own conversion to marxism.

But back to 'historical materialism': since Marx attaches chief importance to Man's role as a producer it is natural that he should regard the mode of production as the main factor reponsible for determining the character of a given society. What he calls the 'ideological superstructure' of a given society—its form of government, its institutions, politics, culture, etc.—is, in his view, basically determined by the mode of production and by the contradictions that arise in the economic field generally. These contradictions, according to him, are also responsible for the general historical development of human society. It was while trying to explain this development that Marx found the hegelian dialectic a useful tool. Hegel conceived of development as a dialectical process resulting from a clash of opposites. In what may be called his 'logical diagram' of development Hegel distinguishes between three main stages: an initial stage or stage of 'affirmation', a second stage or stage of 'negation' and a third stage or stage of 'negation of negation' in which the 'contradiction' between the first two is resolved at a higher level; the latter stage may lead to a new 'negation', and so on. In his own theory of history, Marx retained this idea of dialectical development, but gave it a 'materialist' interpretation. While Hegel spoke of a conflict of dialectical opposites in the progress of 'Absolute Spirit' towards its 'self-knowledge', Marx speaks of a 'clash of contradictions' in the economic and social development of human society; he rejects Hegel's idealistic metaphysics and concentrates on the study of *political economy*.

According to Marx, the dialectical contradictions in the economic and social spheres are due to a conflict between the 'productive forces' and the 'relations of production'; that is, between those directly engaged in production and their capacity to produce wealth, on the one hand, and the general social-political set-up in which they work and which becomes a hindrance to a further expansion of production and a more balanced distribution of wealth, on the other. The result of this conflict, according to Marx, is a *class struggle* which leads eventually to the overthrow of the existing social-political structure. Gradually, new contradictions arise and this leads to a further change, and so on.

The conflict between the productive forces and the relations of production, according to Marx, has become especially acute in capitalist society, with a comparatively small capitalist class holding in their hands the means of production and the large mass of expropriated proletariat denied all real power. This anomalous situation, maintains Marx, will be fully redressed only in a communist society in which the producers themselves will assume full control over the means of production, distribution and exchange and in which, as a result of this, the old conflict between the 'productive forces' and the 'relations of production' will disappear, thus removing all need for classes and class struggle. The setting up of a communist society, according to Marx, will lead to the full emancipation of Man as a free individual. It will mean the end of Man's

own 'alienation' in the present class structure. It will free Man
from his economic and social enslavement, giving him the opportunity of developing all his capacities to the full. Marx's vision of
the communist society was a vision of a 'realm of freedom'. He
spoke of freedom not as something that we already possess but as
a historical goal yet to be attained. Unlike the romantics who maintained that Man can overcome his own 'alienation' and regain his
freedom by returning to the 'standpoint of subjectivity', Marx
maintained that Man will be able to enjoy full freedom in a communist classless society. In short, Marx's view is that if Man is to overcome his own 'alienation' and be able to live an authentically free
existence the structure of *society* must be radically altered.

Sartre's marxism

Sartre has now accepted the basic marxist tenets. Earlier he was
closer to Kierkegaard than to Marx and, as we saw, he insisted
on the 'unobjectifiability' of human subjectivity and on the primacy
of existence over 'objectifying knowledge'. Now he is prepared
to see the human individual as part of a wider historical social
context in which (and with which) this individual develops and
grows. He is prepared to look at Man as an object as well as the
existential subject (of feeling and knowing).

He now puts less emphasis on the individual and more on the
'group'. He analyses social 'aggregates'. (The first volume of his
Critique of Dialectical Reason bears the title 'Théorie des ensembles
pratiques'.) To be sure, there are elements in his earlier philosophy
which might be said to piont in this direction. For one thing, he
never argued in favour of an 'anarchic' idea of freedom. He was
anxious to show that freedom and responsibility necessarily go hand
in hand. My freedom as an individual, he repeatedly emphasised,
is tied up with the freedom of 'others'. I cannot desire freedom for
myself without at the same time desiring freedom for other people.
Freedom is not an unlimited licence to act as one pleases. It involves
certain duties towards other people and their freedom. But while in
his pre-marxist phase Sartre was not quite sure what these duties
were and how they ought to be discharged, now apparently he has
found an answer to this problem.

In *Being and Nothingness*, as we pointed out earlier, he made great
efforts to show that the existence of an individual, my own existence,
is inextricably intertwined with the existence of other people. A
solipsistic existence, he maintained, is an impossibility. I cannot
'escape' from 'others'. I am in a continuous relationship with them.
Without them I would not be what I am. But while from Sartre's
earlier standpoint 'others' seemed to be there only to emphasise

my essential loneliness and to remind me of the gulf between my freedom and their world, Sartre now accepts that myself and 'others' inhabit a common world and that the others in my group can in certain circumstances take my decisions for me. Sartre now analyses the social *milieu* from a more 'positive' aspect. He emphasises the role of collectives and groups and their formative influence on the individual. At the same time, he criticises what he regards as 'dogmatic marxism'. While firmly adhering to basic marxist teachings he thinks that the majority of modern marxists have distorted and formalised marxist doctrine, with the result that no place has been left in it for the individual, the particular. He now accepts, he says, 'without reservations', Marx's view that 'the mode of production of material life generally dominates the development of social, political and intellectual life.'[1] but he rejects what he regards as the narrow and dogmatic interpretation of this principle by modern Marxists. This principle, Sartre maintains, does not mean that Man is no more than a 'sum of conditioned reflexes'—a passive product of his environment. By interpreting the above principle in this way the dogmatic marxists have emptied marxism of all its human content and turned it into an empty formula. Marxism, says Sartre, must be rescued from the dogmatists, and this requires an 'existentialist intervention'. Sartre now appears very much in the role of a marxist Luther, trying to reform a bureaucratised and distorted faith.

The main task of existentialism, as Sartre now sees it, is to 'humanise' marxism, to find a place in it for the individual. Beyond this reformist role existentialism has no other role to fulfil. Marxism, says Sartre, is the 'dominant philosophy' of our age, and existentialism is only an *enclave* inside marxism—an ideology which will disappear as soon as present-day marxism is reformed to incorporate the human elements it has so far ignored.

However, it is not altogether clear how this task of 'humanisation' of marxism is to be accomplished. For although attacking 'dogmatic marxism' Sartre does not give up any of the articles of the Marxist dogma. He regards Marx's historical materialism as 'the only valid interpretation of history' and one wonders what freedom this leaves to the individual except the freedom to accept what the 'dogmatists' have always presented as the only truth.

There is one concept which plays an important role in marxism and which Sartre sees as a link between the existentialist and the marxist position: the concept of *praxis*. According to Marx, the dialectical laws of history work through human *praxis*. *Praxis*, from Marx's standpoint, means in the first place activity in the field

[1] *Critique de la Raison Dialectique* (Paris, 1960), p. 31.

of production, but not exclusively; in an enlarged sense, it includes the social and political as well as the economic activity of Man. Sartre now finds that in his own philosophical analysis of this activity he can re-employ his earlier 'existentialist' concepts without leaving the framework of marxist philosophy. The concept of *praxis*, according to him, is inseparable from that of need. The human *praxis* is an expression of need (in the widest sense) and involves 'transcendence' and 'project'. It involves, that is, a surpassing of the present, of the already existent, and a 'projecting' of oneself towards what is not yet realised or achieved. In *praxis* Man 'projects' himself towards future, towards his own possibilities. He transcends the immediate conditions of his existence and tries to improve or change these conditions. His activity, according to Sartre, must be seen against the background of the 'conditions of scarcity' in which he lives. Man lives and works under 'conditions of scarcity' and it is towards overcoming this scarcity that his *praxis* is directed.

To Sartre, human *praxis* represents a historical process of what he calls 'dialectical totalisation'. The concept of totalisation is another concept which Sartre had already used in his *Being and Nothingness*. But in a marxist context this concept inevitably receives a slightly different meaning. Sartre, we saw earlier, interpreted the For-itself as a 'lack of coincidence with itself'. This lack is permanent and all efforts towards a 'totalisation' of the For-itself are doomed to failure. Now prominence is given to the concept of 'scarcity'. The way in which Sartre talks about scarcity, however, is not free from ambiguity. Is scarcity a permanent feature of the human existence—like the ontological gap within the For-itself—or is it a characteristic of the continuing *historical* situation in which mankind finds itself? Sartre's aim in introducing the concept of scarcity, one may assume, was not simply to replace an ontological category by an economic one. Yet, in an effort perhaps to stay close to Marx, Sartre often refers to scarcity in such a way that its ontological significance becomes obscured. From the marxist point of view, the situation of scarcity is a historical situation which need not last for ever. Marxists visualise a new society in the future in which the needs that now determine our actions and shape the structure of our present society will no longer exist. But one can hardly suppose that the setting up of the new society will change Man's *ontological* situation which, according to Sartre's earlier diagnosis, is charac- terised by a permanent gap within the For-itself due to the For-itself's lack of 'coincidence with itself'. If so, need and scarcity will continue to exist, although they may of course assume very different forms.

This raises the all-important problem of freedom, and, as we shall see presently, reveals very clearly the precariousness of Sartre's new philosophical position. We saw earlier that his interpretation of the 'gap' within the For-itself was closely connected with his concept of freedom. Ontologically, freedom was regarded by Sartre as an expression of the 'unobjectifiability' of the For-itself. The essence of the For-itself, Sartre maintained, is that it 'lacks' itself as an object. To overcome this 'lack' would mean destroying freedom completely. Freedom and 'lack' go hand in hand. From the marxist point of view however (which Sartre now claims to have embraced), freedom is a historical category and should be considered in connexion with the problem of the emancipation of Man from his 'alienation' in the existing class structure. Real freedom cannot be achieved before the structure of society has been radically changed and the conditions of scarcity overcome. We have here, then, two distinct ideas of freedom: one ontologico-existential and one social-historical, and it is far from clear how these two ideas can be united, if this is what Sartre is trying to achieve.

The difficulties involved here will become more obvious if we pursue the contrast between the marxist and the existentialist position a little further.

First of all, the marxist theory of history, historical materialism, is based on a principle of historical necessity. History, according to Marx, is governed by laws which cannot be changed by a deliberate action of any one individual. Its course is determined by what happens in the field of production, and, as far as capitalist society is concerned, its system of production gives rise to contradictions which will lead inevitably—whether Sartre wills it or not—to the overthrow of the capitalist social structure and to the establishing of a classless society. Only then will Man be really free. It is clear that, from the marxist point of view, talk of the 'unobjectifiability' of the human subjectivity and of freedom as the 'essence' of Man without taking note of historical conditions makes little sense, if any at all. However convinced I may be subjectively of being entirely free, I cannot help being conditioned by my environment, and my actions and views will inevitably bear the imprint of my class background. If, on the other hand, my freedom is *not* fictitious, if I am really free (as Sartre's earlier ontological existential analysis seemed to imply) then one may wonder what sense there is in talking of historical necessity. What sense can there be in talking of freedom as a 'historical goal'? When, one day, the (material) scarcity is overcome—as it seems likely it will be—this will of course bring an enormous increase in the *variety of choice,* but the basic ontological structure of 'human reality'—of which freedom, as Sartre earlier assured us, was a constitutive characteristic—will remain unchanged.

The problem, briefly, is this: if we are really free, then marxism is not *necessary*. We may choose to adopt marxism, but we *need not* do so, and no one has the right to blame us for not choosing it. Nor indeed can anyone prove us 'wrong'. If, however, marxism is the voice of History itself, as Sartre now assures us,[1] then our opposing it makes no sense. The only sensible thing for us to do is to accept it. But what remains, in this case, of our freedom?

This, in short, is Sartre's dilemma. He accepts all the basic marxist tenets, including the idea of historical necessity. At the same time, he is not quite willing to give up his own idea of 'subjective freedom'. In his bulky *Critique of Dialectical Reason* in which he expounds his new doctrine he makes great efforts to demonstrate what he calls the 'dialectical unity'[2] of freedom and necessity in *praxis*. Everything is now regarded by him under the aspect of 'dialectical unity': freedom and necessity, existence and knowledge, particular and universal. But since the process of 'historical totalisation' meanwhile goes on regardless, it is not clear what elbow room this alleged unity leaves to me as an individual. Am I free only to accept what is necessary? What is the significance of my 'subjective freedom'? Sartre says that the individual has a definite role to play within marxism. But what role? What grounds can I find in my individual *praxis* for accepting the idea of *one* history and *one* truth? And if it so happens that I do not find any sufficient reason for accepting a marxist commitment, why should anyone have the right to judge me in the name of a 'historical necessity' which I have good reason to doubt and to reject? Sartre gives no clear answer to any of these questions. All he does is to insist on the 'dialectical unity' of freedom and necessity. But this is a very obscure concept which his *Critique* has not made a whit clearer, and I suspect that he himself is at a loss what meaning precisely should be attached to it.

---

[1] 'Le marxisme, c'est l'Histoire elle-même prenant conscience de soi'. *Critique de la Raison Dialectique*. p. 134.
[2] ibid., p. 131.

14

THE LIMITATIONS OF PHENOMENOLOGY—
CONCLUDING REMARKS

Sartre's adoption of marxism was an attempt on his part to extricate himself from a difficult situation in which he had found himself as a result of his phenomenological analysis of consciousness. We saw that his analysis led him to draw a distinction between the conscious mode of being and the correlative non-conscious mode characteristic of the world of objects, and to maintain that consciousness harbours 'nothingness' within itself. 'Human subjectivity' was found by him to be an inexplicable pool of 'negation' in *being*. Man had freedom but his freedom seemed only to expose his homelessness and the 'absurdity' of his existence. Freedom meant being alone with one's decisions; it meant a permanent 'existential transcendence' over every 'external' set-up, system, theory; freedom was a permanent reminder of the 'unobjectifiability' of 'human subjectivity'. This was the result of Sartre's existential-phenomenological analysis and it was obvious that along this road he could not get very far in explaining such simple things as how a man can be referred to perfectly legitimately in the third person and true judgements made about his behaviour and his experiences. Sartre claimed that 'subjectivity' was his point of departure. But from the standpoint of subjectivity, not unnaturally, only the 'domain of subjectivity' can be seen, and from the standpoint of 'existential subjectivity' only that of 'existential' subjectivity. In order to be able to see beyond the confines of 'existential subjectivity' Sartre had to change his standpoint. He had to widen the basis of his analysis, and this, as we pointed out earlier, meant in fact introducing certain assumptions which could not be justified in purely phenomenological terms, and thereby indirectly admitting the *inadequacy* of the phenomenological approach. An example of such an assumption is the marxist proposition that the mode of production of material life generally dominates the development of social, political and intellectual life, which, as we saw, Sartre now unreservedly accepts.

Sartre found several useful points of contact between existentialism and marxism. One of them was the emphasis that both existentialism and marxism place on action as against mere theorising, on involvement as against academic detachment and aloofness from everyday life. The existentialists join the marxists in rejecting what might be called the 'Aristotelian' view of philosophy. The latter view, to which, incidentally, Husserl still fully subscribed, is the view of philosophy as an eminently contemplative theoretical activity, *theoria*. The existentialists, on the other hand, regard philosophy as a form of existential commitment and, generally, as something much more directly concerned with life and the problems of the 'human condition'. They reject the idea of philosophy as an 'academic pursuit'. They are against 'interpretation without action' and this is why Sartre, for one, finds marxism appealing. They are against academic system-building, but—less attractively—they combine their opposition against academic theorising with a strong anti-rationalist bias.

Anti-rationalism has been a distinct feature of all existential phenomenology. Husserl's 'intellectualism' was soon abandoned in favour of a 'phenomenology of emotions'. All phenomenologists from Scheler to Sartre attached the greatest importance to an analysis of emotions. They all regarded a descriptive analysis of emotions to be philosophically more profitable than a logical analysis of knowledge. But although united in their opposition to philosophical rationalism, they often disagreed among themselves considerably in many other respects. Whereas the German phenomenologists showed strong metaphysical and mystical leanings, Sartre and like-minded existentialists close to him were often provocatively atheistic. The phenomenological 'metaphysicians' tended to see Man and his freedom as part of a wider metaphysical plan within which Man had a definite mission to fulfil. For Sartre, as we saw, there is no such 'metaphysical plan'. Sartre entirely rejects the idea of a mystical 'Absolute'. There is no God for Man to turn to. Man, according to Sartre, is free and utterly alone. Man gives meaning to everything; he is the judge of everything. He alone is responsible for his own future. However, the immediate question was *how* to act and *what* decisions to take, and here, as we saw, Sartre could offer no real guidance. What do we do with our freedom? How do we preserve it? What political stand should we take in the actual

situation in which we find ourselves today? These questions deman-
ded concrete answers. Albert Camus thought that in order to assert
and preserve our freedom we should resist most vigorously all
'totalitarian ideologies' as well as go on attacking the hypocrisies
and injustices of bourgeois society. In his view, 'revolutionary
trade-unionism' (this 'negation of bureaucratic and abstract centra-
lism', as he calls it) is a good political example of such an attitude.
But to Sartre this 'revolutionary trade-unionism' smacked of social
pragmatism, and after years of indecision he settled for Marx.

From Husserl's transcendentalism to Sartre's existential dialectic
it is a very long way and yet Sartre's difficulties were in many
ways symptomatic of the whole 'phenomenological school'. The
idea of 'presupposition-less' philosophising had to be abandoned
if one wanted to increase the explanatory power of one's philosophical analysis. This was the general conclusion that the phenomenologists seemed to be confronted with and it is not difficult to
see why.

Characteristically, all phenomenologists find it difficult to cope
with two important problems: the problem of clarifying the status
of science and scientific knowledge in relation to philosophy and
the problem of 'other people' (the so-called 'problem of others').
Although phenomenology did not begin as an anti-scientific movement the fact is that the 'phenomenological school' turned progressively against science. There is no doubt that this was due in part
to a lack of real understanding of the method of deductive reasoning
from hypotheses (explicit presuppositions) on which science depends.
We saw that irrationalist tendencies gradually prevailed inside the
'phenomenological school' with the result that an unabridgeable
gulf was created between philosophy and science. Phenomenologists
not only abandoned the ideal of a 'science of science' which Husserl
still pursued, but were anxious to underline what they regarded
as the philosophical inferiority of scientific methods compared with
the 'existential dialectic'. Their antipathy to what Sartre calls the
'analytical reason' rose in direct proportion to their interest in
existential paradoxes. Sartre's own philosophy is the best example
for this, and there is no doubt that his own antipathy to 'analytical
reason' made his adoption of marxist dialectic much easier.

Then there is the 'problem of others'. We saw that Husserl himself
struggled, largely unsuccessfully, with this problem. After he had
performed his phenomenological reduction one of his biggest
problems was to explain the possibility of 'other egos'. He had to
explain how 'others' can be reached from the monadic position
of his 'transcendental Ego'. Empirically the existence of other
people is a fact of which I am immediately aware. But the empirical

certainty I have of the existence of 'others' is part of that 'natural attitude' which I am asked to suspend. According to Husserl, I must perform the phenomenological reduction, i.e. put the 'natural world' into which the 'others' belong between 'brackets'. This done, I must attempt a 'phenomenological constitution' of 'others', i.e. try and explain the possibility of their existence in an *a priori* way. But it is difficult to see how I can ever discover in this way other egos equal in all respects to myself.

The unsurmountable difficulties of a 'phenomenological constitution' of 'others' on a transcendental basis was one of the reasons why other phenomenologists largely abandoned the doctrine of the 'transcendental Ego' and tried to avoid the dangers of solipsism by widening the basis of their phenomenological analyses. We saw that Scheler, for example, replaced the concept of the 'transcendental Ego' by his concept of a 'person' and that, to him, a person was the centre of both intellectual and emotional acts. Scheler was very anxious to emphasise the importance of 'social emotions' in the life of a person. And yet, from his position, the existence of 'others' remained a somewhat puzzling fact. What had to be shown was that the existence of 'others' is in an absolute sense constitutive of my own existence as a person, and Scheler failed to prove this in a convincing way. Heidegger too was faced with the same problem. To be sure, he maintained that 'being-with-others' is a constitutive fact about *Dasein*; the modus 'being-with', according to Heidegger, is part of the modus 'being-in-the-world' which characterises *Dasein*'s manner-of-being. But the curious fact is that this 'being-with' is manifested in a sphere which in Heidegger's philosophy comes under the category of 'inauthenticity'. We find 'others' in what to Heidegger is the impersonal 'they-sphere' of *das Man*— in a sphere, that is, in which according to him the real truth about ourselves remains hidden from us. His view is that in order to be able to discover this truth we must respond to the 'call of conscience' and 'return to ourselves', that is, to our own 'interiority'. It is only as *ek*-sistence, he says, that *Dasein* lives in the 'proximity of being'. But the trouble is that, on this view, I can it seems live in the 'proximity of being' only as an individual and not in a community with 'others'. Sartre, for his part, tried to solve this difficulty about 'others' by attempting to show that the 'others' are so inextricably woven into the texture of my being that they cannot be either 'lost' or ignored. But in spite of all his efforts the problem remained basically unsolved, for the 'others', in the context of his existentialist philosophy, seemed only to underline my essential solitude and to increase the problems which my freedom continually creates for me. The presence of 'others' had largely a negative function of reminding me of my inescapable situation as a free and lonely individual. Sartre was himself aware of the inadequacy of his solution, and his subsequent conversion to marxism was another attempt on his part to solve this excruciating problem.

But the difficulties which they all had to face, their inability to solve the 'problem of others' and their lack of understanding of science, can all be traced back ultimately to the same roots. There is a view which they all basically accept and which goes back to St Augustine. *Noli foras ire,* wrote Augustine, *in te redi, in interiori homine habitat veritas.* 'The truth is not to be found in the external world; it resides in the interiority of Man'. The phenomenologists begin their analyses with this 'interiority', although their interpretations of this 'interiority' may vary considerably. In Husserl's philosophy, as we saw, this interiority becomes 'transcendental subjectivity'. In Scheler's philosophy, it is the interiority of the person and his acts (although Scheler tried subsequently to break the barriers of 'interiority', first in a platonist and then in a kind of pantheistic metaphysics). In Heidegger's philosophy, it is the interiorised 'truth of being'. In Sartre's philosophy, it is the 'existential subjectivity'. They all look for philosophical truth in the human interiority just as Descartes did before them, although most of them do not accept Cartesian rationalism or Cartesian metaphysics.

It is inevitable that the belief that truth resides in the interiority of Man should create a 'problem of others' and also raise the problem of the status of science. For how can I, from my own interiority, penetrate into the interiority of 'others' and recognise them as fully equal to myself? And if truth resides in the 'interiority' of Man what value and what importance should be attached to the 'external', 'public' facts with which science is concerned? These problems immediately impose themselves upon us and demand an answer. They also raise the wider question about what the nature of philosophical inquiry ought to be. Can philosophy afford to confine itself to a phenomenological 'analysis of interiority'? Might it not be possible to dispense with the 'standpoint of interiority' altogether? Perhaps neither is possible or desirable. But how can philosophy bridge the gulf between the internal and the external, private and public? What criteria should it follow, what methods should it use?

The philosophers whose views we have been discussing in the preceding pages attach central importance to the phenomenon of *intentionality*. They concentrate on the analysis of 'intentional experiences', for, in their view, it is through an analysis of these experiences and not through any accumulation and analysis of 'external' data that a philosophical understanding of the world

and of ourselves becomes possible. We saw that Husserl's philosophical development was largely determined by his adoption of
intentionality as a guiding principle, and that because of his adoption
of intentionality he came into conflict with Frege. Frege was a
logician whose guiding principle was the principle of logical equivalence. He studied the problem of interchangeability of expressions;
he was interested in definitions and the criteria of indentification
of logical entities. Husserl, on the other hand, was interested in
what he called the 'origin' of the concept of number. He used
Brentano's theory of intentionality as a basis for an explanation
of this 'origin', and although he later dissociated himself from
Brentano's 'psychologism' his early adoption of intentionality
remained a decisive factor in his philosophical development. It
was his interest in intentionality that led him to phenomenology,
and to that phenomenological *interiority* which became the source
of so many excruciating problems for him and for his many followers.

However, Husserl maintained that by withdrawing to the position
of the phenomenological interiority one need not abandon the ideals
of objectivity and universality, provided this interiority was interpreted in the right way, that is, as a 'transcendental subjectivity'.
He wanted to develop phenomenology as a 'strict science' on a
transcendental basis. His analysis, from his standpoint, was just
as rigorous as Frege's own. But while Frege was guided in his analysis
by the principle of logical equivalence, Husserl relied on intentionality. His approach was different, and so inevitably was his conception
of facts. He studied what he regarded as the objective facts arrived
at through an intuition of the 'essential structures' of intentional
experiences. In this, his view clearly differed from the view a scientist,
say, a physicist, might have of facts. His facts were neither logical
nor empirical, but *phenomenological*. Nevertheless, he claimed
for them a scientific status.

To Husserl, intentionality was a key to these phenomenological
facts. But if intentionality had revealed this new region of facts,
it was not very clear in what sense precisely these facts should be
regarded as scientific. Nor was it quite clear how the ideals of scientific objectivity and universality can be achieved on the basis of a
phenomenological analysis of intentional experiences. For after
all, the phenomenological method developed by Husserl proved to
be compatible with different philosophical standpoints, and we saw
that the so-called 'phenomenological school' included philosophers
who showed very little interest for, or understanding of, science.

Husserl himself abandoned his early mathematical studies, and
his attitude towards natural science and its methods became increasingly critical as he went on developing his own phenomenological

method. In all this one problem played a decisive role: the problem of meaning. It was the intentionalist theory of meaning that formed the basis of phenomenology and determined the course of its subsequent development. The fundamental thesis was that the 'phenomenon of meaning' cannot be explained in terms of reference of expressions, or in terms of the truth-value of statements, or in terms of rules, written or unwritten, for the use of signs, but that it involves, and requires an analysis of, a *meaning-giving act*. Once this was accepted, what was more natural than to turn to the source of these 'acts', to Man, and to examine the nature of his 'interiority' and his peculiar manner-of-being? This is precisely what the philosophers of existence have done. However, they have turned even further away from science in the process.

But there are two features of the 'phenomenological position' which may nevertheless appeal to the scientifically minded philosopher; they are, first, the attempt to overcome the traditional conflict between idealism and materialism, and, secondly, the rejection of the doctrine of substance. We mentioned Husserl's stubborn insistence on 'facts'. His great ambition was to confine his analysis to what he regarded as objective facts and to avoid all doctrinal disputes. The business of phenomenology was not to take sides in the materialism *versus* idealism dispute but to analyse as objectively as possible the essential structures of our intentional experiences. It is interesting that the philosophers of existence also tried to preserve this neutrality. They tried to present their own existential analysis as an 'objective' description of straight facts without committing themselves to either side in what they considered to be a purely metaphysical dispute. The phenomenologists, as we pointed out in the introductory chapter, are very anxious that their analyses should be accepted as being free from any metaphysical bias. They claim to provide a completely unprejudiced analysis of facts, beginning from the most simple immediate experiences. But it is only just to add that while making this claim they nevertheless take it for granted that what they regard as facts are not explicable in terms of 'external' empirical facts, and that intentionality is an absolutely indispensable instrument of a philosophical inquiry.

The second and perhaps more interesting feature of the 'phenomenological position' is its rejection of the doctrine of substance. The majority of phenomenologists are united in their rejection of the traditional doctrine of substance, and, although their method is in many ways reminiscent of that employed by Descartes, they are in this respect anti-Cartesian. They reject the doctrine of substance not only because what is traditionally meant by 'substance' remains forever outside the domain of possible experience, but because the whole idea of substance suggests something complete in itself and static, something that is 'incapable of having a future'.

The rejection by the phenomenologists of the materialism/idealism dispute and their rejection of the doctrine of substance are a direct result of their criticism of metaphysical dogmatism which, as we pointed out earlier, shows a certain similarity of attitude between them and the logical positivists. But there the similarity ends and disagreements begin. Phenomenology, especially German phenomenology, in spite of its insistence on the neutrality of its method, shows a consistent tendency to develop in a metaphysical direction. Its whole approach to the problems of meaning and truth is very different from a positivist approach to these problems. Let an example taken from Heidegger illustrate this.

The positivists maintained that the key to meaningfulness lies in the possibility of *verification*, i.e. in the possibility of establishing whether something is or is not the case. But what exactly is involved in verification?—asks Heidegger. What does it mean to say that a statement is *true*, or that it is *not true*? Imagine a picture on the wall and someone facing away from it, remarking: 'The picture on the wall does not hang straight.' Suppose this is true. What does this 'truth' consist in? In a correspondence between what is said and what is the case? But how do we establish this correspondence? The object referred to in the above statement is the picture on the wall and it is said about this picture that it does not hang straight. This statement reveals something about the picture in relation to *ourselves*. The important thing which usually escapes notice, says Heidegger, is that a true statement does not *reflect* a fact, but *shows* it. Truth, he maintains, involves an 'act of disclosure' and this inevitably points to the presence of an existent who lives in a disclosing way, i.e. Man. There is truth, says Heidegger, only as long as there is *Dasein*. The way to the facts about the world leads through *Dasein*. 'Newton's laws, the principle of contradiction or any other truth'—he writes—'is true only as long as there is *Dasein*.'[1] Consequently, we should concentrate on the analysis of *Dasein*, for *Dasein*, according to Heidegger, is the source from which the word 'truth' ultimately derives its meaning. To a logical positivist who interprets 'truth' as verifiability of certain propositions within a certain system on the basis of certain rules all this of course does not mean very much, if anything at all.

But whether Heidegger's approach makes sense or not, whether it can be justified or not, one thing is undeniable. His existential phenomenology was a sign of the evaporation of the interest in logic and logical problems which was the driving force behind much of

[1] *Sein und Zeit*, p. 226.

Husserl's early analysis and was shared by a number of philosophers influenced by him. Other issues began to occupy phenomenologists. The emphasis was shifted from transcendental phenomenology such as Husserl was propounding to existential phenomenology. One of the results of this development, as we saw, was a marked trend towards irrationalism and an increasing estrangement of phenomenology from science. Science was criticised, its methods dismissed as inadequate, and, at the same time, science was feared. Phenomenologists seemed to have found a common cause with a number of philosophical anthropologists, mystics and philosophers of culture all of whom were issuing warnings about the dangers that modern science brings to Man. In the years following the First World War there was much talk about a 'crisis of culture'. The war seemed to cast doubts on the whole idea of progress. The destruction and the turmoil of the war years created an atmosphere of disillusionment and the future was viewed with increasing apprehension. The war had not yet ended when the Bolshevik Revolution broke out in Russia, an event which was to have such far-reaching repercussions for the whole world. Many European intellectuals who saw science being exploited for war purposes voiced their fears about the consequences of its further abuse. Technical civilisation with its fetishism of the machine seemed to bring a destruction of cultural values in its wake. In 1918 Oswald Spengler published the first volume of his famous book *Decline of the West* in which he prophesied a downfall of western culture and which was widely read by intellectuals in the post-war years. As a result of the influence of this book it became increasingly popular to contrast culture with technical civilisation and to regard the latter as a potential menace to cultural values. There is a discernible echo of such an attitude in Scheler's and Heidegger's distinction between *Spirit* and technical (or as they also sometimes call it, scientific) intelligence, and in their championing of the cause of *Spirit*.

The intellectual climate after the Second World War showed similar features to that following the First World War and the popularity of existentialism on the European Continent in the post-war period must be seen against the background of a widespread feeling of disillusionment, uncertainty and concern for the individual in an age of technocracy and political regimentation; an attitude of mind not unlike that which caused a considerable number of intellectuals to view 'technical intelligence' and its fruits with suspicion some twenty years or so earlier. Once again the phenomenological method seemed to offer the most adequate means of countering the 'presumptions' of 'technical intelligence' and 'analytic reason'. Once again the phenomenologists found themselves confronted with their old rivals and staunch defenders of science, the logical positivists.

But if there is one general conclusion that we must draw from our analysis so far, it is simply this. Whatever else the phenomenological method may accomplish it cannot provide a basis for a 'presupposition-less' phenomenological philosophy and in so far as the phenomenologists make this their aim their efforts are bound to end in failure. The mere fact that they often disagree among themselves points to the different presuppositions of their analyses. Moreover, they are, as we have seen, often driven to widen the bases of their analyses by introducing additional assumptions which are neither self-validating nor reducible to those which are. But if such a widening of the basic assumptions becomes necessary then much of the criticism directed against deductive reasoning from non-self-validating premisses loses its force. This granted, the problem of a 'philosophical beginning' presents itself in a new light. It becomes clear that it is useless to look for a 'safe' Cartesian platform within the domain of 'subjectivity' from which to start our philosophising, for there is no such platform. What is necessary is to decide on a minimum number of basic premisses, bearing in mind the different aspects of reality, and work from there.

SHORT BIBLIOGRAPHY

The following list is a selection of books available in English. Foreign editions are quoted in the text.

HUSSERL

Logical Investigations, trans. J. N. Findlay (London, Routledge & Kegan Paul, 1970).
The Idea of Phenomenology, trans. William P. Alston and George Nakhnikian (The Hague, Martinus Nijhoff, 1964).
Ideas, General Introduction to Pure Phenomenology, trans. W. R. Boyce Gibson (London, Allen & Unwin, 1958).
Cartesian Meditations, trans. Dorion Cairns (The Hague, Martinus Nijhoff, 1960).
Formal and Transcendental Logic, trans. D. Cairns (The Hague, Martinus Nijhoff, 1969).

SCHELER
The Nature of Sympathy, trans. Peter Heath (London, Routledge & Kegan Paul, 1970).

HEIDEGGER

Being and Time, trans. John Macquarrie and Edward Robinson (London, SCM Press, 1962).
An Introduction to Metaphysics, trans. Ralph Manheim (Garden City, NY, Doubleday & Co., 1961).

SARTRE

Being and Nothingness, trans. Hazel E. Barnes (London, Methuen, 1957).

Existentialism and Humanism, trans, Philip Mairet (London, Methuen, 1963).

The Problem of Method, trans. Hazel E. Barnes (London, Methuen, 1963).

OTHER BOOKS

Marvin Farber, *The Foundations of Phenomenology* (Cambridge, Mass., Harvard University Press, 1943).

E. Parl Welch, *Edmund Husserl's Phenomenology* (Los Angeles, The University of Southern California Press, 1939).

E. W. Ranly, *Scheler's Phenomenology of Community* (The Hague, Martinus Nijhoff, 1966).

A. R. Manser, *Sartre* (London University Press, 1966).

W. D. Desan, *The Marxism of Jean-Paul Sartre* (Garden City, NY, Doubleday Anchor Books, 1966).

M. Merleau-Ponty, *Phenomenology of Perception,* trans. Colin Smith (London, Routledge, 1962).

INDEX

ABSTRACT IDEAS, 56 ff.
Abstraction, 28
  theories of, 56 ff.
  ideating abstraction, 62 f., *see
    also* Ideation
Act, 28, 30 f., 43, 45, 47 ff., 52,
    56, 67 f., 70, 91 f., 100, 125
  ascetic act, 100
  emotional acts, 93, 96
  meaning-fulfilling acts, 53 f., 67
  meaning-giving acts, 52 f., 67,
    81; *see also* Ideation,
    Reduction
Analyticity, 38
Angst, 117 ff.
Augustine, St, 149

BAD FAITH, 130
Being, 104 ff., 113, 116, 120, 123,
    127, 129
  being-for-itself, 132, 137
  being-for-others, 95, 132
  being-in-itself, 127, 137
  being-in-the-world, 116, 118
  non-being, 108–10, 128 f.
Berkeley, 15 f., 28, 57–60, 66
Bracketing (method of), 71, 73,
    77, 79, 82 f., 100

Brentano, 23, 29, 45–50, 108
  and Husserl, 23, 29, 50
  Brentano's psychologism,
    50

CALCULUS, 26
Camus, A., 132, 147
Care, 116, 118 ff.
Carnap, 18
Category, 36
  pure meaning-categories, 36 f.
  pure object-categories, 36 f.
Causality, 86 f.
Collective, 28 f.
Collective association, 29–31
Complexes of sensations, 66
Conditional reflex, 98 f.
Connexion
  perceptual, 30
  primary, 30
Conscience, 120
Consciousness, 11, 48, 50, 70
  cognitive, 17, 79
  empirical, 'psychological', 70
  intentional, 70
  intentionality of, 50
  object-constituting, 92
  reflective, 19